PLATO

The Instructional Design Library

Volume 30

PLATO

Harold F. Rahmlow
The American College
Bryn Mawr, Pennsylvania

Robert C. Fratini
Western Electric Company
Dublin, Ohio

James R. Ghesquiere
Control Data Corporation
Baltimore, Maryland

Danny G. Langdon
Series Editor

Educational Technology Publications
Englewood Cliffs, New Jersey 07632

Library of Congress Cataloging in Publication Data

Rahmlow, Harold F
   PLATO.

   (The Instructional design library; v. 30)
   Bibliography: p.
   1. PLATO (Electronic Computer System)
2. Computer managed instruction. I. Fratini,
Robert C., joint author. II. Ghesquiere, James R.,
joint author. III. Title. IV. Series:
Instructional design library; v. 30.
LB1028.46.R33   371.39'445   79-26395
ISBN 0-87778-150-8

Copyright © 1980 Educational Technology Publications, Inc., Englewood Cliffs, New Jersey 07632.

All rights reserved. No part of this book may be reproduced or transmitted, in any form or by any means, electronic or mechanical, including photocopying, recording, or by any information storage and retrieval system, without permission in writing from the Publisher.

Printed in the United States of America.

Library of Congress Catalog Card Number: 79-26395.

International Standard Book Number: 0-87778-150-8.

First Printing: March, 1980.

FOREWORD

Computers—in and of themselves—are not instructional designs. Rather, they are one of the media channels available for transmitting information. The decision to include some form of computer-based instructional designs in the *Instructional Design Library* was not an easy one. One option was to describe computerized instruction in the general manner of computer-assisted and computer-managed instruction. The problem is that such an orientation would lack specifics for application. Thus, a decision was made by the Series Editor and publisher to describe and illustrate two specific and widely used computer systems and, within these systems, the specific instructional design(s) which maximize the unique features of the computer medium. The computer system described in this book is the widely used PLATO system.

PLATO is the nation's most widely used computer system for instruction. In this book, you will find an excellent description of both computer-managed and computer-assisted instruction within the general framework of computer-based education. PLATO has several unique features for guiding instruction that other instructional designs are incapable of, and these features are illustrated for the reader. Having worked with PLATO on a limited scale myself, I am pleased to say that computerized instruction is finally beginning to achieve many of the benefits ascribed to it.

Danny G. Langdon
Series Editor

PREFACE

The authors appreciate the opportunity to contribute some thoughts on PLATO* to the readers of *The Instructional Design Library*. We wish to acknowledge and thank the thousands of persons at the University of Illinois, Control Data Corporation, and elsewhere who have made PLATO a reality and continue to advance its capabilities.

Special thanks go to two persons: Dr. Michael W. Allen, an architect of PLATO learning management, who provided many constructive comments on the manuscript; and Lillian G. Pedrick, a colleague at The American College, who has been an integral member of The American College courseware development team and who, in this capacity, has contributed to our writing of this book. Finally, we wish to acknowledge the contribution of Barbara Faulkner in the preparation of numerous drafts and the final manuscript.

Thanks also go to Danny G. Langdon, Series Editor. Without his prodding, this book would still be a set of scattered notes!

H.F.R.
R.C.F.
J.R.G.

*PLATO® is a Registered Trade Mark and Service Mark of Control Data Corporation. Used by permission.

CONTENTS

FOREWORD v

PREFACE vii

ABSTRACT xi

   I. USE 3

   II. OPERATIONAL DESCRIPTION 17

   III. DESIGN FORMAT 35

   IV. OUTCOMES 61

   V. DEVELOPMENTAL GUIDE 69

   VI. RESOURCES 91

   VII. APPENDIX 95

ABSTRACT

PLATO

PLATO is a large-scale computer-based education system. It provides an effective means for developing and delivering programs of individualized education. Simultaneously, PLATO can use a wide variety of instructional designs to deliver courses in a variety of learning areas to large numbers of students.

PLATO can be used for managing instruction or as an instructional medium in its own right. It can be used as an adjunct to classroom instruction or as a medium for delivering interactive, independent instruction. PLATO allows geographical as well as temporal flexibility, while maintaining an identity of quality.

PLATO

I.

USE

This opening chapter sets the stage for the remainder of the book by briefly describing PLATO and by providing the context in which PLATO is used. The significance of PLATO as a tool for individualizing education is stressed. Uses of PLATO are examined from the point of view of the student, the instructor, and the author. The chapter discusses computer-assisted instruction and computer-managed instruction. Examples which will be carried throughout the book are introduced.

The PLATO system described in this book is not a single system; rather, it is a set of systems which are identical in origin, design, and function. There are different released versions, but all are being upgraded and maintained at the same level. PLATO systems are large-scale computer-based educational delivery systems, each with the capability to also perform functions such as cataloging, storage and retrieval of information, composing and text-editing, the calculation and graphic display of statistical information, and other specialized tasks. Although PLATO can perform a number of tasks, it is important to remember that it was originally designed specifically to serve as a computer base for the delivery of a variety of instructional strategies in any number of learning areas. The Appendix to this book provides a brief history of

PLATO. PLATO is a Registered Trade Mark of the Control Data Corporation.

Danny G. Langdon, Editor of *The Instructional Design Library,* of which this book is a component, has defined an instructional design as a "prescription of the necessary events and activities of learning which provide a *guidance* function toward the achievement of specific objectives and the promoting of desired learner capabilities." While PLATO does fulfill the requirements for an instructional design, it can perhaps be thought of more easily as a powerful tool for the presentation or delivery of a variety of instructional designs. Because of the capabilities of the computer system which is PLATO's "heart," PLATO both creates its own unique instructional designs and expands the power of other instructional designs that do not necessarily have to be based on a computer.

Facilitating Individualization

PLATO Systems

Each PLATO system is designed with a single, central computer that can support hundreds of simultaneous users working at independent computer terminals. Each can be interacting with a different program, or at different points in the same program; but because of the computer's speed and time-sharing ability, each terminal receives individualized "attention," and students can be unaware that they are actually sharing the computer with hundreds of other users. *PLATO thus can be seen as a means for the simultaneous individualized delivery to many students of a variety of instructional designs in a number of learning areas.*

Persons interact with the standard PLATO terminal via a touch-sensitive screen over a cathode ray tube (CRT) and a typewriter-like keyboard as shown in Figure 1; however, the terminal and the computer have the capability to support

Figure 1

PLATO Terminal

such external devices as random-access audio devices, speech synthesizers, hardcopy units, optical scanners, and random-access videodiscs. Furthermore, since the display screen has the capabilities to both present high-resolution graphics and interpret touch inputs to various sectors of the screen, interaction with PLATO is not limited to only those students who have the ability to read and/or type. PLATO's versatility in presenting instructional designs and accepting student interaction is the reason for its usefulness at almost all levels of education.

PLATO is ideally suited to simulation, especially when high-quality graphics are significant. Simulations can be used as teaching tools for concepts for which there may not be a high degree of student motivation; for example, the teaching of arithmetic computational skills as is done in the PLATO lesson, *Speedway*. Simulations are also extremely useful for teaching skills which involve a degree of danger or expensive equipment; the chemistry simulation described in this book as well as flight training programs developed by the airlines are examples.

PLATO possesses those mechanical and logistical features normally associated with computers which suit it well for drill and practice, tutorials, problem-solving, and computational activities. An example in *The Mathematics of Life Insurance* is developed later in this book.

On a more comprehensive scale, PLATO can be used as a vehicle for computer-managed instruction (CMI). Operating in this mode, it provides an eclectic CMI tool as will be seen in the example developed later.

PLATO can be utilized effectively by learners at virtually any age level. While the use of typing skills is required for some applications, the touch panel enables the circumvention of the keyboard.

PLATO is not an appropriate tool for the teaching of motor skills or for capabilities involving extensive oral communication. It could, however, be used to *direct* the learning of such capabilities.

Teachers will be discussed herein from two points of view: (1) the authors of educational materials and (2) the instructors or administrators of educational programs. A single individual often plays both roles.

Student Use

From the student's point of view, PLATO is used to individualize instruction in several different ways. First, the computer can be used to offer a variety of modes of instruction to the student, depending on the student's preference or abilities. Second, PLATO can be used to offer the student a variety of response modes and response-judging features. Not only can PLATO offer the student several modes by which the student may indicate his or her response to a problem posed by the computer, but PLATO can also tailor messages and subsequent learning choices to the student's particular response at this point in the educational program. This leads to a third type of individualization that PLATO can offer to the student. This is the ability to individualize broad lesson choices, depending on the student's mastery of certain material, the student's own choice to go on, or some combination of these two criteria.

Teacher Use

For the author, PLATO can be used to develop, present, and evaluate a variety of instructional designs in a broad spectrum of subject-matter areas. The author works directly with the computer system in the design and programming of lesson material; when students subsequently use the PLATO lessons, data can be collected on student performance, and problem areas identified can be eliminated. This use of PLATO will be treated in greater detail in the Developmental Guide chapter.

An instructor can use PLATO to administer and track student progress through instructional materials and to locate materials developed in other parts of the country or world that would be of use to students. PLATO contains an on-line catalog with information that can be searched by the instructor that will help determine whether a lesson in a particular subject area is indeed appropriate; in addition, some PLATO systems publish a printed catalog of available lessons. Once the instructor provides students with access to a particular lesson, he or she can use any PLATO terminal to monitor individual student performance and/or the entire class's progress as a whole. The system automatically provides summary information on student performance and also offers the teacher the capability to either send students personal messages or see at his or her terminal exactly what the individual student is seeing.

Examples

As examples of instructional designs that can be presented via PLATO, two instructional programs and one overall instructional design will be presented and further developed in subsequent chapters of this book. As an example of simulation, *Acid-Base Titrations,* a college-level chemistry experiment/lesson, will be discussed. As an example of an instructional strategy which we will refer to as "tutorial drill and practice," we will examine *The Mathematics of Life Insurance,* a course for professional-level adult learners. And, as an example of an instructional design which was developed to simplify the use of PLATO, we will examine PLATO learning management, Control Data Corporation's term for their computer-managed instruction system.

Terminology

The terminology and acronyms associated with computers and education are numerous and often confusing. The term "computer-based education" (CBE) is the broadest and most generic. It is used to mean any education activity in which the computer plays a significant role. The term "computer-assisted instruction" (CAI) is employed to mean the use of the computer as an instructional medium. As an instructional medium, the computer takes its place with the classroom teacher, films, television, audiotape, and other resources. The term "computer-managed instruction" (CMI) designates the use of the computer as a learning management tool. Both CMI and CAI are subsumed under the generic term, CBE.

Confusion in terminology exists primarily because these terms are not mutually exclusive but in fact represent a multidimensional continuum. To illustrate, consider the administration of a test. Is it an instructional or management function? Probably some of each. Consider a branching, programmed instruction sequence. Does it not perform both an instructional function and a management function? Certainly, functions do exist which can be classified as highly management oriented; i.e., test scoring, recordkeeping. Likewise, certain functions can be classified as highly instructionally oriented, i.e., presentation of reading, simulation.

In reality, then, we will use the term CBE when referring to generic educational activity related to computers; we will use the term CAI when referring to activities for which the instructional component dominates; and we will use the term CMI when the management component dominates.

When referring to the Control Data Corporation's computer-based education programs, another unique set of terminology exists. Control Data refers to its computer-assisted instruction as PLATO-assisted learning and to its computer-managed instruction as PLATO learning management.

Computer-Assisted Instruction

Background

Although the term computer-assisted instruction can be used to describe a broad category of instructional designs involving learning as the ultimate result of interaction with a computer, for our purposes, computer-assisted instruction (CAI) will be limited to only those instructional designs where interaction with the computer is the direct basis for student learning. This does not mean that a CAI design cannot take advantage of learning resources in a variety of media, but only that interaction with the computer forms the core learning experience for the total learning environment. Despite this narrowing of the criteria for CAI, the instructional designer has great freedom to choose and implement instructional strategies because of the flexibility of the TUTOR programming language—the language used to create computer-assisted instructional designs for PLATO.

The flexibility of combining a variety of instructional strategies employing student interaction with a computer is the major advantage of PLATO-assisted learning. If there is a question concerning the students' learning needs, computer-assisted instructional designs can incorporate assessment lessons and learning prescriptions similar to those available through PLATO learning management. However, the needs assessment mechanism is not an integral part of PLATO-assisted learning. If the students' learning needs are already known, students can go directly to learning activities involving questions posed by PLATO to which the students must provide answers. The amount of input required of the student can be varied from considerable, where the student is required to make a response in order to proceed from step to step in the learning process, to little, where the computer functions basically as an electronic page-turner requiring only occasional input from the student. Learning strategies requiring considerable interaction are ideal for computer-based applications. This is because of the computer's patient ability to lead the student through the steps in a learning process, over and over again if necessary, until the student has indicated mastery of the material. Combining activities with varying amounts of interaction with a computer-managed learning assessment and recordkeeping system can result in a total computer-based education environment for the student.

As one might expect, in order to take advantage of the flexibility of PLATO in constructing computer-assisted instructional designs, one must become fairly proficient in the TUTOR language. PLATO contains a number of features and instructional lessons designed to assist the novice programmer, and the expertise required to program a simple computer-assisted lesson can be acquired with a few days of study. But one should be aware that more sophisticated PLATO-based instructional designs will require a more in-depth understanding of the intricacies of TUTOR.

The primary use of PLATO-assisted learning for the student is to provide a totally individualized instructional environment. Interaction with PLATO will be at the center of the student's learning experience. Although PLATO's questioning and the student's responses to those questions will be the primary means by which learner interaction takes place in a computer-based instructional design, the computer can also serve as instructional manager and refer the student to other noncomputer-based learning activities in order to provide the student with a complete and well-balanced instructional unit. Individualization for the student results from interaction with PLATO and is designed so that the next step in the student's instructional sequence is dependent on the student's response to the question posed at each step. Although this may sound very similar to simple programmed instruction, computer-based lessons can be designed to simulate a variety of learning conditions and provide a number of student-branching alternatives not readily available in other modes of individualized instruction.

CAI provides authors freedom to implement a variety of interactive instructional designs in combination to form a total instructional unit. The instructional design can be perfectly tailored to meet the precise demands of the particular learning need, providing as many or as few learning activities as are required for the student to achieve mastery of the subject.

PLATO-assisted learning can be designed to provide the instructor with detailed information on the students' progress through the interactive learning activities. This information is valuable not only for assessing the students' progress at various points as they move through the curriculum, but also for evaluating the effectiveness of the computer-based lessons themselves. Such recordkeeping truly makes it possible for one to revise lessons according to the kinds of hard data that are much more difficult to obtain when other media are used.

Examples

The use of PLATO-assisted learning will be illustrated further throughout this volume through a discussion of *The Mathematics of Life Insurance* and through a discussion of *Acid-Base Titrations*.

The Mathematics of Life Insurance

The Mathematics of Life Insurance is a 15-hour computer-based curriculum designed to assist students seeking the CLU (Chartered Life Underwriter) professional designation from The American College. The course helps students learn to apply the principles involved in the development of life insurance premiums, nonforfeiture values, reserves, surplus, and dividends. This course was chosen to serve as an example because of the variety of computer-based instructional strategies it employs to provide the student with a thorough understanding and a certain level of comfort in working with the subject matter. The course can be used by students on the campus of The American College, in Control Data Learning Centers, and other organizations and institutions having access to the CDC PLATO network.

Acid-Base Titrations

Acid-Base Titrations is an undergraduate level topic which is usually about one-fifth of a full semester course. This PLATO lesson, which was written by Dr. Stanley Smith, Professor of Chemistry at the University of Illinois, contains a presentation of the theory section, a drill and practice section, and a laboratory simulation section.

The theoretical material is used as a supplement to the classroom lecture, a supplement to the textbook, and as a review for the PLATO drill and practice section. The drill and practice section is used by the instructors as a replacement for traditional "quiz/discussion" classroom time. Since the students receive a "score" for the PLATO activities, the drill and practice section also serves as a replacement for homework assignments.

The laboratory simulation section is used as a preparation for the actual laboratory experiment. In this simulation, the student must set up equipment, perform the experiment, and analyze the results. After gaining the experience with the PLATO simulation, the student spends less time doing the actual laboratory experiment. In addition, the student is more cognizant of the chemical reactions occurring in the laboratory as the experiment progresses.

The *Acid-Base Titrations* material on the PLATO system is used by numerous colleges and universities throughout the country. It is also being used for training technicians in the industrial sector as well.

Computer-Managed Instruction

Background

One of the most cost-effective uses of computer-based education is for the individualization of education and instruction. The history of computer-managed instruction dates back to the mid-1960's. Among the more notable early systems was Individually Prescribed Instruction (IPI) developed by Cooley and Glaser at the Learning Research & Development Center at the University of Pittsburgh. More comprehensive in scope was Project PLAN, which was conceptualized by John C. Flanagan and jointly developed by the American Institutes for Research, Westinghouse Learning Corporation, and 13 participating school districts. PLATO learning management is an outgrowth of these and other CMI projects. The primary use for PLATO learning management is for the individualization of education and for the individualization of instruction. Although the terms individualization of education and individualization of instruction are used interchangeably, the term individualization of education is meant to be more encompassing and includes the tailoring of a curriculum or set of instructional objectives for a student as well as the tailoring of the instructional method for teaching those objectives.

The student uses PLATO learning management in a variety of ways to assist in tailoring a program of individualized education. Students are given guidance in the selection and sequencing of learning objectives through the use of testing procedures. Students complete test items related to specific objectives and, based upon the results of those tests, are provided with prescriptions for study materials. Specific learning resources may be prescribed for students, or students may be given flexibility in their choice of learning resources. Students also use PLATO learning management to keep a record of their progress. Information provided to students includes not only information on materials mastered, but also information on materials that have been worked on but not mastered, the time tests were taken, and the sequence in which the materials have been studied.

PLATO learning management also assists the author in the development of computer-managed instruction materials. Its format or structure is generic. The author does not have to be an expert in computer technology to develop a course. The author does need to have the capability of developing objectives, designing objectives-based test items, and matching learning resources with objectives. PLATO learning management, however, supplies the structure within which the teacher can implement computer-managed instruction.

The structure available for use by the author includes formats with respect to testing strategies, the specification of learning resources to match objectives, and data to monitor student progress. These data are very beneficial to the developer during the formative stages of the courses. The developmental feature is, in fact, significant enough that it is worthwhile for teachers to use PLATO learning management to develop and test instructional materials, even if the ultimate delivery system for the materials is not to be computer-managed instruction.

The instructor's use of PLATO learning management is quite similar to the use of PLATO in general. The instructor can review previously developed learning resources. The instructor can select materials for student use, can assign prerequisite requirements, and can provide specific guidance in assisting students in choosing learning resources. In addition, the instructor can monitor student progress in the study of a course.

Because of the generic nature of PLATO learning management, it can be used for virtually any subject at any level. Knowledge of computer programming is not required. There are, however, some reading difficulty problems in its current version which make it difficult for students without adequate reading capability to utilize the system. The authors feel that this is not an insurmountable problem and that it is one likely to be overcome in future versions.

Examples

The use of PLATO learning management will be illustrated through two examples: (1) the flight training program at United Airlines and (2) by The American College in its course development work.

United Airlines Flight Operations Training utilizes PLATO learning management in the training of newly hired pilots. The course of training that would have taken four weeks using conventional instructional methods is being completed in an average of nine days. The American College is currently using PLATO learning management as a developmental tool for its graduate course in *Research Methods*. One end-result of this work will be a set of printed materials for students not having access to PLATO.

Summary

PLATO is a powerful computing system designed specifically for educational applications. PLATO can be used effectively as a management tool (as illustrated in PLATO learning management), or it can be used effectively as an instructional medium (as illustrated in the discussion of PLATO-assisted learning). PLATO provides a means for individualized delivery, to many students simultaneously, of a variety of instructional designs in a number of learning environments.

II.
OPERATIONAL DESCRIPTION

This chapter describes the operational characteristics of PLATO and how they interact from the point of view of the student, the author, and the instructor. The major focus of the discussion will be on the student. The chapter also includes a discussion of the administrative operation of the PLATO system itself. Finally, the two sample PLATO instructional programs and the instructional design introduced in Chapter I are developed so as to exemplify the operational characteristics and to set the stage for elaboration in the Design Format chapter, which follows this chapter.

All PLATO systems are manufactured by Control Data Corporation but are owned or operated by a number of organizations. In addition to the systems operated by Control Data, other systems exist at the University of Illinois, Florida State University, the University of Delaware, the University of Quebec, and in Brussels. Most of these systems interconnect for communication and transfer of lessons. The versatility of PLATO can be evidenced, in part, by noting that the preceding list includes major universities, a profit-making organization which is international in scope, and a system in which the majority of the instruction is in French. However, the majority of the features of these separate systems are generic rather than unique to a particular PLATO system.

Operational Characteristics

Student

The student interacts with the PLATO system through a terminal. Two types of terminals are in general use: the Information Systems Terminal (IST) and a Plasma Terminal. From the point of view of the student, the differences between these terminals are for the most part cosmetic, and the text will not go into technical detail concerning the differences between them. The terminal consists of a visual display screen which looks like a black-and-white television screen and keyboard. Figure 1 in Chapter I shows a PLATO terminal.

PLATO is an interactive system providing personal attention. The student receives information visually through the display screen; or, in some cases, he or she may receive information through an auditory channel. In the case of visually displayed material, the material may consist of printed letters of a variety of type fonts as well as static graphics and animation. The graphics capabilities of the terminal enable straight lines as well as curves of almost any configuration to be displayed, and the graphics motion capability is limited only by the creativity of the author. In the case of the use of audio, such as is employed in the music program at the University of Delaware, a random-access audio urrit and a music synthesizer are attached.

The student responds to the system either through the keyboard or by touching the screen. The keyboard is a standard typewriter keyboard with additional function keys added. If a student is familiar with the ordinary typewriter, operating the PLATO keyboard presents no problems. If the student is not familiar with a typewriter, the author can rely more heavily on the terminal's touch feature. Communication with the touch feature of the PLATO terminal is accomplished by actually touching the display screen. The

Operational Description

screen is divided into 256 touch-sensitive addresses or locations, and specific locations can be used to communicate specific information. To illustrate a very simple use, consider the administration of a multiple-choice test. Rather than typing a response on the keyboard, the student could touch the correct response on the screen. In addition, using touch the student can move items from one location on the screen to another. This is particularly useful if the student is asked to rearrange items that appear in a display, such as words in a sentence, items belonging to a given set, or the assembly of equipment used in a chemical simulation.

Author

The author communicates with PLATO in the same way the student communicates, although the purpose is different. An author wishes to communicate with the system in order to develop curriculum materials.

To accomplish the development function, the author types text and program code into the computer in the same way he or she would use any typewriter, except that the capabilities for editing copy are vastly superior. Static graphics and blocks of text can be developed even without knowledge of the TUTOR language which generates the displays. Once material has been entered into the system, the author can recall the information and see the lesson as it would be presented to a student.

In addition to the actual development of course materials, the Control Data PLATO Network offers additional features which can be of great assistance to an author. Using the communications capabilities of the system, the author can converse instantaneously with other authors. Communication with other authors can take the form of two types of notes. One type is readable by a number of authors on the system, and a second type is accessible only by a specific individual author. That is, an author in Philadelphia and an author in

Los Angeles can type messages to each other and, in turn, read each other's messages simultaneously, with the additional option of one author being able to monitor the other author's screen display, if they so desire. So, although an individual author may be sitting in isolation, he or she does, in fact, have the opportunity for interacting with other professionals on a nationwide basis.

Not only may an author consult with other authors, but also an author may consult with system consultants. These are professionals in the use of PLATO who are available on the system to consult with authors having problems. Such a consultation service is highly valuable and can save a great deal of time in the development process.

Instructor

The instructor uses the PLATO system for administrative purposes as well as for counseling. The PLATO system keeps records on individual student progress, and the information may be accessed either on an individual student basis or a group basis. The instructor function will be elaborated upon in the next chapter.

Administrative Operation

PLATO terminals may be used alone or in conjunction with a wide variety of other instructional resources. Computer-managed instruction illustrates well the integration of instructional resources.

Catalogs

Courses available on each PLATO Network are listed in an on-line catalog. The inventory may be accessed by course title, author, or content. The course descriptions are stored in a hierarchical manner so that the user can access the level of information desired about a course without having to review all information available on that course.

Networks

Although a number of PLATO systems have been installed, they all have common features. All operate with a large computer in a central location. Users are connected to the large computer by phone lines, microwave communication, video channels, and via satellite to Europe. For example, the University of Illinois system has its main computer in Illinois and has users located throughout the world. Likewise, a Control Data PLATO System is located in Minnesota and also has a network of users worldwide. PLATO systems are also linked together so that information contained in one system can be accessed or transferred to another.

The use of large computer networks has advantages and disadvantages. The primary advantages to the user are access to a very large, sophisticated computer, data bases, and a wide communications network. This network means that curriculum materials can be disseminated to students throughout the world simultaneously and that economies of scale can be obtained by widespread use of existing materials. In addition, modifications or improvements in course material can be implemented simultaneously and quickly on a worldwide basis. On the other hand, the primary disadvantage with a large computer network, such as PLATO, is its vulnerability to communications problems and the expense of the communication. Severe storms or other natural disasters can raise havoc with telephone communications and can render the system inoperative. Fortunately, however, such major problems occur infrequently and are usually corrected within a few hours.

The technique of "down-loading" can be of assistance in alleviating some communications problems, as follows: A student could dial into the central computer. The computer in turn would, through a high-speed communication link, send material to the terminal at which the student was working. The student would then disconnect from the main computer and use his or her own terminal for computer-assisted instruction work. When the student was finished doing his or her work, he or she would again call the main computer and feed back any necessary information. This concept has a number of advantages including the cost saving of not having to maintain communication links for an extended period of time, and also, the potential minimization of communications problems.

Examples of PLATO Programs

To further clarify and exemplify the operation of PLATO, two general categories of programs will be discussed. First, two examples of computer-assisted instruction will be presented. Second, PLATO learning management, PLATO's operation as a computer-managed instruction system, is described. Within this second section, brief mention is made of applications by United Airlines and by The American College.

Computer-Assisted Instruction

When PLATO operates in a computer-assisted instruction mode, the primary medium of instruction is PLATO itself. Two examples of such a design will be discussed. First, detail is given on a course in *The Mathematics of Life Insurance*. Second, a brief description of a course in *Acid-Base Titrations* is presented in order to illustrate additional aspects of computer-assisted instruction.

This section will describe the way in which PLATO-assisted learning operates as an instructional design, using The American College's course in *The Mathematics of Life Insurance* to illustrate various design features. These features can be combined to make up an entire curriculum where the PLATO activities provide the core of the instruction.

A student begins *The Mathematics of Life Insurance* by working through three preliminary lessons:

Operational Description

(1) the first orienting the student to the layout of the PLATO keyboard and the special uses of certain function keys;

(2) a second describing the features and giving the student practice in the use of the touch-activated calculator available on the display screen when answers to problem situations involve complex calculations; and

(3) a third describing the components of *The Mathematics of Life Insurance* PLATO course, explaining mastery criteria, and offering the student suggestions on which CAI activities may best meet certain specific student needs.

The three lessons are listed at the top of Figure 2.

Before the student begins any part of the mathematics content itself, he or she is given a complete orientation to interacting with the PLATO computer, certain special features of the particular instructional program, and an overall view of the instructional components and how they fit together to form a comprehensive course. Since few students bring extensive experience in interacting with a computer to their first instructional session, such a complete orientation helps the students feel more at ease, with much less anxiety in anticipating what to expect. Mastering new and difficult subject matter is hard enough without having to learn an entirely foreign instructional medium, which PLATO is to the majority of the students. If the student is already familiar with PLATO, he or she is required to complete only the lesson describing the components of the specific course before choosing a lesson in *The Mathematics of Life Insurance* curriculum.

The Mathematics of Life Insurance is a complete computer-assisted curriculum in that PLATO provides the student with a number of instructional alternatives and provides him or her with suggestions rather than forced choices. Although

Figure 2

Instructional Design for
The Mathematics of Life Insurance

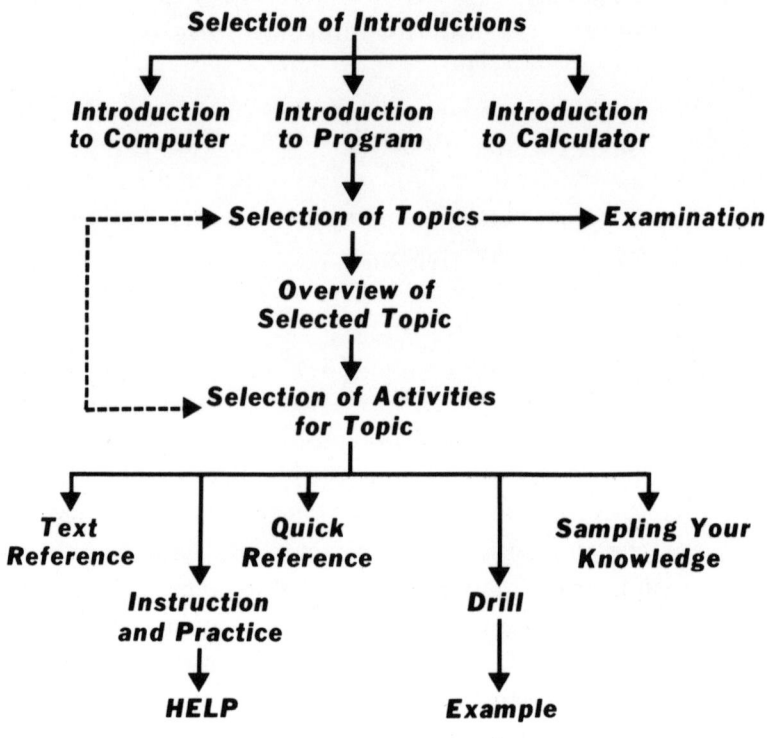

the designer may program the lesson to facilitate the student's choosing the alternative the designer would prefer, it is especially important for adult learners to feel that they, and not PLATO, make the instructional decisions. In this way, it is truly computer-*assisted* instruction rather than computer-*controlled.*

The first decision that a student must make in *The Mathematics of Life Insurance* is which of the 11 content areas to study. Figure 3 illustrates the computer display the student would see. After the student chooses one topic from the main index of topics that appears on the PLATO display, the display provides the student with an overview of the topic stating the learning objectives of that particular portion of the course. After reading the overview, the student is given the choice of choosing another topic or proceeding to work on the one already chosen.

The student is then given the opportunity to indicate his or her mastery of a specific topic by completing a ten-item quiz, known as Sampling Your Knowledge, at a 90 percent or 100 percent level of mastery. This brief quiz consists of true/false and short completion type items or problems taken from the range of content of the topic. The student has four types of instructional resources available to him or her on PLATO to assist in achieving mastery of the Sampling Your Knowledge quiz. One resource, Text Reference consists of page references in the textbooks used for the course (as offered, in this example, by The American College). A second resource is known as "Quick Reference"; it provides short definitions and examples of specific concepts covered by the topic and allows the student the option of reviewing a specific definition or of paging through all the definitions and examples for the topic. "Instruction and Practice" provides the student with short segments of instruction and then asks the student to apply that instruction by solving problems based on the information just presented. The fourth CAI resource,

Figure 3

Topic Index

```
************************************
*        The Mathematics           *
*              of                  *
*        Life Insurance            *
************************************


   a    Probability Concepts

 → b    Mortality Concepts

   c    Interest Concepts

   d    Net Single Premiums

   e    Net Level Premiums

   f    Policy Reserves

*******************************************page 1 of 2

   g    Your Status in the Curriculum
```

Choose a letter, or press one of these keys:
   SHIFT-STOP to sign off
   BACK for previous lessons | NEXT for more lessons |
   HELP for explanation   LAB to read or send notes

From the Control Data PLATO® course, *The Mathematics of Life Insurance,* Copyright © 1978 by Control Data Corporation. Used by permission.

Operational Description

"Drill," provides the student with randomly-generated problem situations covered by the topic; the student can do as many or as few drill problems as he or she desires, since he or she can leave Drill whenever he or she so chooses. The student still has a large bank of potential problems available should he or she desire several hours of practice in the topic. Figure 4 shows a sample index of CAI instructional resources taken from the topic, "Mortality Concepts."

Once the student has indicated mastery of the 11 subject-matter topics by scoring 90 to 100 percent on the ten-item test for each topic, the student is eligible to access a PLATO activity that simulates the conditions the student will face in taking the national examination offered by The American College. The student is provided with 25 objective test items of the item type used by The American College in its national examinations and receives no immediate feedback as to the correctness of his or her responses (unlike the other interactive PLATO instructional activities). However, at the halfway point and at the end of this practice examination, the student is given feedback based on both his or her use of time (how well he or she is pacing himself or herself) and his or her mastery of specific content areas within the course material, so that the student can give additional attention to the areas of indicated weakness.

Thus, the student's role in participating in *The Mathematics of Life Insurance* computer-assisted curriculum requires him or her to undergo mastery assessment in a number of content areas within the course as a whole, and then to choose learning resources, both PLATO-based activities and materials in other media, to help him or her achieve content mastery. Although PLATO provides the student with suggested learning activities based on the student's test performance, the decision of whether or not to accept PLATO's (actually the instructional designer's) recommendations is always up to the student.

Figure 4

Activity Index

```
┌─────────────────────┐
│   M O R T A L I T Y │
│   C O N C E P T S   │
└─────────────────────┘
```

Choose any activity you wish. Remember that completion credit for this topic is given only for successful performance on Sampling Your Knowledge.

Choose a letter:

→ a.   Text Reference

→ → b.   Quick Reference

    c.   Sampling Your Knowledge

    d.   Instruction & Practice

∗ e.   Drill

Or press SHIFT-STOP to choose a new topic;
          BACK for an Overview of this topic;
          HELP for an explanation.

From the Control Data PLATO® course, *The Mathematics of Life Insurance,* Copyright © 1978 by Control Data Corporation. Used by permission.

Operational Description

The Mathematics of Life Insurance PLATO curriculum was designed to offer the student complete freedom of choice in selecting learning activities. However, to provide students with some sort of guidance, the lesson authors did provide suggested paths through the materials for three broad categories of students: (1) the "introductory" student, who enters the course with no prior knowledge of the subject matter; (2) the "supplemental" student, who is using PLATO in addition to some other form of instruction (such as a formal class) on the subject matter; and (3) the "review" student, who wishes to use PLATO to identify gaps in his or her overall mastery of the subject after having studied the material extensively in some other mode at a previous time. These paths and their design implications will be discussed in more detail in the Design Format chapter. Before closing the discussion of this sample program, a few brief statements need to be made about the role of the author.

The role of the author can be divided into three basic tasks: (1) to decide on the instructional design features and criteria to be employed in the particular PLATO curriculum; (2) to develop the course material to appear on PLATO in a script-like format; and (3) to generate the TUTOR program-language code to generate that course material on the PLATO terminal. All three of these processes, plus a fourth role, testing, will be covered in extensive detail in the Developmental Guide chapter.

An instructor using *The Mathematics of Life Insurance* curriculum would have two major responsibilities: (1) to track student mastery of the various content topics in the course to insure that students are moving through the course at an appropriate rate; and (2) to use PLATO's data-collection capabilities to identify areas of the PLATO learning activities that are not meeting students' learning needs and to suggest ways of revising those areas.

A second sample program, *Acid-Base Titrations*, will

exemplify other uses and design features capable of operating in the PLATO system. Its most notable characteristic is the integration of computer-assisted instruction with laboratory activities. Students use PLATO for presentation of theory, drill and practice, and laboratory simulation. The student may study chemistry at a designated time in the chemistry building. However, many times it would be more convenient to study the chemistry materials in the evening at a different location, such as a library or a residence hall. This flexible scheduling is a reality with the PLATO system. At the University of Illinois, students are able to use PLATO up to 22 hours a day and even 20 hours a day when maintenance is being performed. Not only *can* students use PLATO virtually round the clock . . . they *do*!

Computer-Managed Instruction

We turn now to the use of the computer primarily as a manager as contrasted with a medium of instruction. The computer-managed instruction system which will be discussed is PLATO learning management.

The following operational description of PLATO learning management will be considered from the point of view of the student, the author, and the instructor. Several definitions of terminology will need to be introduced to understand PLATO learning management.

There are four primary building blocks. These are the instructional unit, the module, the course, and the curriculum.

The curriculum is the largest entity. Curricula are constructed using courses as building blocks. Courses, in turn, are constructed from modules. Each module is, in turn, made up of instructional units and a list of learning resources. An instructional unit consists of objectives, test items, and feedback. The next chapter on design format provides additional detail on the structure of each of the building

Operational Description

blocks. The following will briefly focus on the interaction of students, authors, and instructors with the various components of PLATO learning management.

Figure 5 provides an overview of the interrelationship between authors, instructors, and students. In the top of the figure, it can be seen that authors create modules. The instructors build courses and curricula from modules created by the authors. Students use the courses and curricula constructed by instructors.

Operationally, students may view the structure of a course and preview modules and objectives. Figure 6 provides an overview of the use of a PLATO learning management module by students. Students are first tested on module objectives. If all objectives for a module are not mastered, the student selects and utilizes learning resources covering unmastered objectives. It should be noted that there need not be a one-to-one relationship between learning resources and objectives, but rather a given learning resource may cover a set of objectives or may cover only one objective. After the student has utilized learning resources for study of those objectives not mastered, another test is administered and the cycle continues until the student reaches mastery on all objectives.

Within this process, students have the option of viewing a course structure, previewing modules and objectives, taking tests, receiving prescriptions, and seeing management information on their own progress. In addition, students can leave messages for their instructor and receive messages from the instructor.

Authors are involved in the development of modules. This work includes:
- developing objectives;
- developing objectives-based test questions;
- developing introductions to the module topic;
- developing module descriptions for instructors and authors;

Figure 5

PLATO Learning Management User Modes

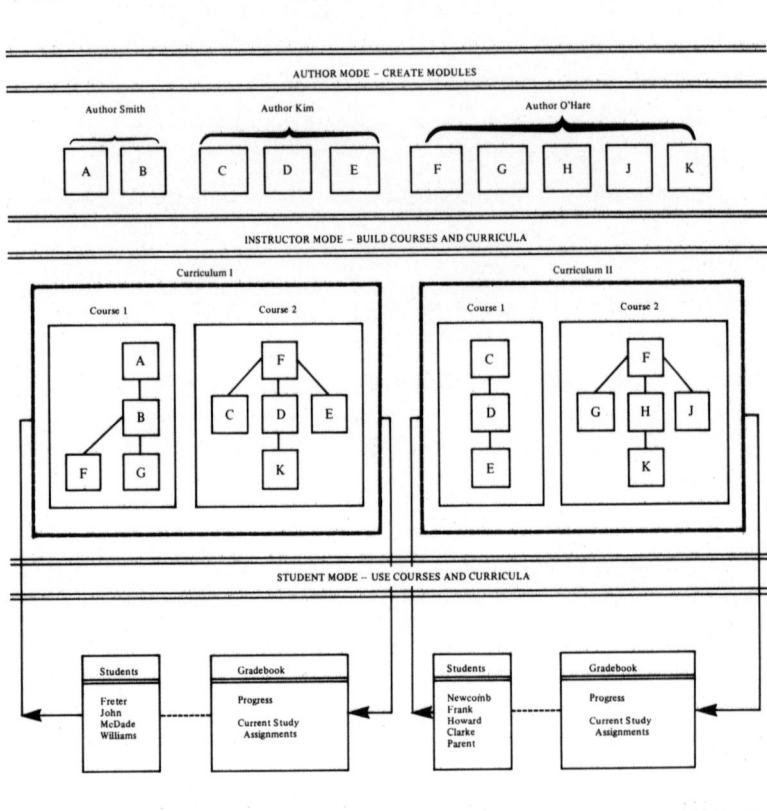

Figure 6

Individualized Instruction Flowchart

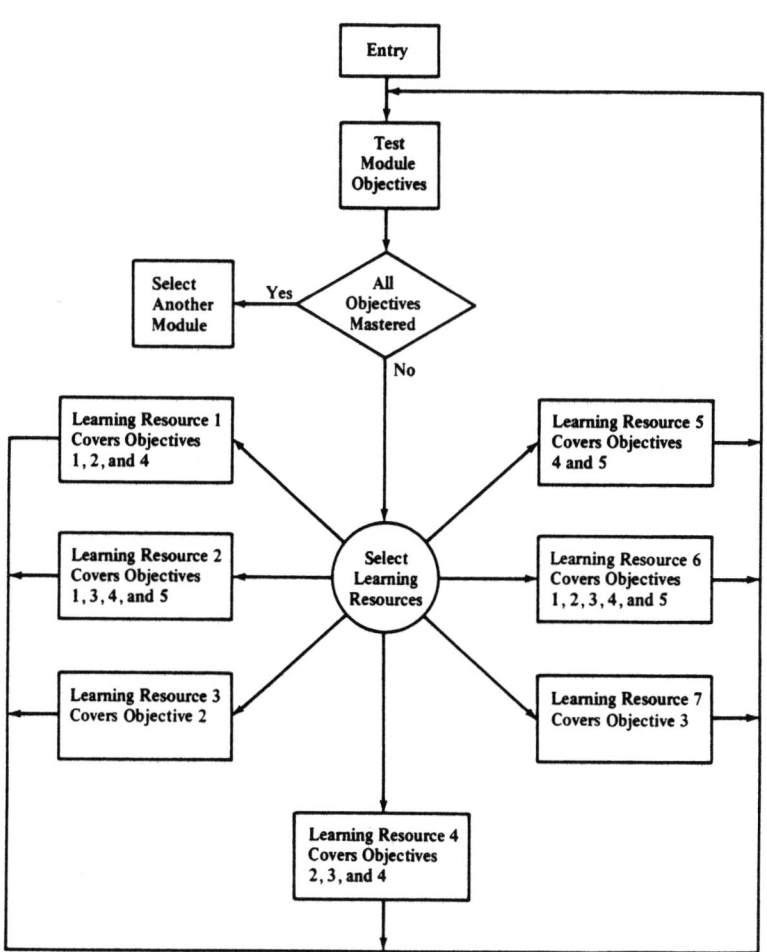

From *A Report of PCMI: PLATO Computer-Managed Instruction,* Copyright © 1980 by Control Data Corporation. Used by permission.

- generating a module title;
- developing feedback messages for mastery and non-mastery of each module objective;
- developing feedback messages for mastery and non-mastery of an entire module;
- specifying test generation parameters;
- developing test scoring specifications; and
- generating and reviewing module tests and reviewing modules written by other authors.

The instructor's primary function is to select and administer curricula to students. In performing this function, the instructor can review and inspect previously developed modules. The instructor can:

- select modules for student use;
- order modules;
- assign prerequisites for modules;
- designate modules as optional or required;
- review module scoring values and testing procedures and modify if desirable; and
- define up to seven management strategies and assign each student to an appropriate strategy.

As an example, United Airlines Flight Operations Training utilizes PLATO learning management in its Denver flight training center. Students interact with the PLATO terminal in a special testing area. Learning resources for the course include audio, video, and print material. As another example, students participating in the computer-managed instruction course at The American College study in their home, office, or at The American College, and come to the College to take tests and receive feedback from the PLATO terminal. In addition, the CMI version of the *Research Methods* course has been made available to selected students at PLATO sites other than at The American College. Use of these additional sites allows for greater diversity in the collection of student-use data.

III.

DESIGN FORMAT

The initial portion of this chapter will describe the design format of PLATO from three points of view:
   (a) system architecture,
   (b) student terminal, and
   (c) student use.

With these general descriptions of the PLATO design format in mind, three specific examples are then presented. These examples should be useful in exemplifying the flexible design characteristics of PLATO as well as serving as possible models for similar needs the reader may be faced with meeting. The examples cannot hope to present the full range of designs that can be utilized. They will present and illustrate, however, many of the most commonly used format components.

System Architecture

A PLATO system is a combination of terminals, a communications network, and a Control Data computer. Data come from a terminal and are directed to the computer through communications channels; based on these data, the computer sends a particular response back to the terminal. These communications channels can be through cables, open-air broadcast, or satellite transmission. A single, central computer can handle up to 32 individual sites, each with up to 32 PLATO terminals. One central computer can, theoretically, simultaneously handle approximately 1,000 terminals; however, in actual practice there may be a degradation of response time when more than one-third of that number of terminals are used simultaneously. A detailed discussion of the central computer of a PLATO system is beyond the scope of this book; it should be noted, however, that the heart of a PLATO system is a Control Data Cyber computer. These systems are able to access and rapidly process vast amounts of information. The structure of the PLATO system allows response time to each terminal to be relatively unaffected by the number of terminals on the system.

Student Terminal

The Information Systems Terminal (IST) and the Plasma Terminal have similar characteristics. For the purpose of this chapter, only the newer IST will be discussed. The IST is an interactive computer-graphics terminal with an 8.5 x 8.5 inch display screen consisting of a 512 x 512 matrix of randomly addressable points (262,144 points). The screen can accommodate 32 lines of alphanumeric characters with 64 characters per line. Standard characters or special font characters of the author's own design can be used. Individual portions of the screen can be selectively written upon or erased. When selective addressing is coupled with selective erase, characters can be drawn, erased, and repositioned in rapid succession to produce animation. In addition to the high-resolution cathode ray tube display, the terminal has a touch-sensitive panel, an electronic keyboard, a microprocessor with 6K words of Read Only Memory (ROM) and up to 16K words of Random Access Memory (RAM); and two external input/output jacks are provided to enable attachment of additional devices such as audio devices or screen display printers.

Student Use

A student desiring to take a course is enrolled by an instructor in the curriculum or "group" containing the specific computer-based lessons the student is to study. The sign-on consists of having the student type the name he or she wishes to be known by on the PLATO system, the name of the student's "group," and a unique identifying code of at most ten characters. This code is made up by the student and may be so confidential as to be known only to the student to provide security for the student's records. Once a simple sign-on is completed, the student may continue at any time using lessons for which he or she is authorized.

Students who are new to PLATO are given an orientation to the system. Orientation lessons are standard on PLATO and are referenced in an on-line catalog. A short CAI lesson introduces students to PLATO and to the PLATO keyboard by taking them step-by-step through the operation of the keyboard and the screen. In many courses, the student is allowed to have access to the introduction any time he or she wishes. This enables a student who has not been using the system for some time to refresh himself or herself on its operation. In most cases, however, courses written on PLATO are self-explanatory, and it is not necessary to return to the introductory material.

Most courses on the PLATO system are highly interactive and require a great deal of student participation. Unless the timing feature is used to automatically change displays—a very rare occurrence—students must make a response in order to proceed from one display to the next and thus set their own pace through lessons. In most cases, the response has a meaningful relationship to the learning process.

Designs for Computer Interaction

Although almost every lesson on PLATO represents a unique instructional design, there are several broad categories that can be delineated to provide some idea of the range of interactive instruction that can be delivered via PLATO. Many lessons contain some combination of these designs to provide students with different types of learning experiences, or use several lessons utilizing different instructional designs over the same topic to construct a computer-based course of instruction.

Furthermore, almost all of these computer-based designs can be integrated in one way or another with study materials of other media, such as print, slides, audio, or video. In its purest form, this results in a design, such as PLATO learning management, where the computer may simply manage the students' interaction with other forms of instruction. However, where PLATO CAI lessons are being designed to treat topics already covered by existing study materials, it is practical to reference these other materials in the PLATO lessons and thus provide students with additional learning alternatives at no additional developmental cost.

Integrating other instructional media with PLATO also makes it possible to take advantage of particular strong points of other media. For example, while the PLATO screen is capable of displaying high-resolution graphics, certain applications require nothing less than the precision of detail contained in a photograph. Although the use of such an adjunct medium runs counter to the centralized distribution of computer-based learning provided by a system such as PLATO, in certain applications it is perfectly acceptable to provide individual students with printed supplemental materials for their reference while working on PLATO. Other media, such as audio, can be directly integrated with computer-based lessons through the use of an accessory audio device or can be integrated just as simply as through building references to specific audiotapes into computer-based lessons. The idea is to provide instruction in the most appropriate media for the application; PLATO is just one medium, and

Design Format

by combining PLATO with other media, an innovative instructional designer can construct a learning package that is equally effective for a wide range of students.

Drill and Practice

One specific design can be designated drill and practice, since this design, in its most basic form, consists of the computer providing the student with problem situations and with feedback based on the student's response. This is not to be confused with a testing situation. In drill and practice, the student faces no performance criterion, and the objective is to provide the student with skill in handling a wide variety of problems. A variation on this design is the *Instructional Game*, where problems are presented in the context of a fictional situation, and the performance criterion (if any) is non-threatening in terms of the subject matter. Using the well-known game of "Hangman" to provide students with drill in vocabulary would be a good example of such an application.

Simulations

As instructional games become more sophisticated, they begin to cross over into the realm of instructional design known as simulation. In this design, PLATO attempts to present a real situation in as much detail as possible, changing variables in the situation to reflect student choices and responses to show the student the outcomes of his or her responses. The most difficult part of implementing simulation-type instructional designs is identifying the range of variables and determining how each will be affected by a particular response. Even a simple situation quickly becomes complicated when exposed to such analysis. However, the computer provides capabilities for such simulations that can be matched only by extremely complicated interpersonal interaction, while providing a number of advantages unique to the computer. These advantages include:

- PLATO can provide students with unlimited opportunity to explore the outcomes of a variety of responses in simulation situations;
- PLATO simulations may be less expensive than real-life work, as well as simulating situations where the wrong response in real life could literally be deadly to the student; and
- PLATO can provide simulated experience to students who might not otherwise receive real-life experience.

The *Acid-Base Titrations* lesson discussed in this book is a good example of a simulation that possesses a number of the advantages of such a design.

Representation

Representation is another design that can be well implemented on PLATO. It is similar to a simulation in some senses but differs in that its primary purpose is to show the student an internal process in stop-motion so that the student becomes familiar with the process taking place. An example of a representation might be a lesson that shows the student the flow of current through the various components of an electronic circuit. Representation-type designs lend themselves best to delivery via computer systems, such as PLATO, which feature detailed graphic capabilities to depict components in the process on the display screen. In addition, PLATO's animation capabilities make it possible to construct lessons containing smooth, animated flow from one component in the process to another. Representations can then be combined with other instructional designs to provide the student with opportunities to demonstrate his or her understanding of the process depicted in the representation.

Tutorial

Providing the student with instruction and then asking him or her to apply what he or she has learned is the basis for yet

Design Format

another instructional design on PLATO, the tutorial. Because of PLATO's graphics, animation, and audio capabilities, instruction can take the form of a number of media in addition to text-reading presented on the terminal display screen. Asking the student to then answer questions on the material or solve problems requiring application of the material serves two purposes: it reinforces the student's learning by providing him or her with an opportunity to work with information in some kind of practical sense, and it provides the student with an opportunity to indicate to the teacher that he or she has indeed internalized the information that was presented.

PLATO Learning Management

PLATO learning management (or more generically, Computer-Managed Instruction, or CMI) is indeed an instructional design unto itself. Although it is discussed in detail throughout this book, it is presented here to suggest that it be considered for use in combination with other instructional designs in the construction of a PLATO-based course of instruction that makes the most efficient use of the students' study time.

Examples of Design Formats

Now let us see what some of these designs mean and look like in terms of specific examples.

PLATO-Assisted Learning

The Mathematics of Life Insurance. The overall design of The American College's course in *The Mathematics of Life Insurance* was shown in Figure 2 of Chapter II. Figure 7 focuses on just those aspects of the design dealing with *The Mathematics of Life Insurance* itself. Once a student has completed the overview of the course, a subject-matter index is presented. Upon selecting a topic for study, the student is presented a choice of activities.

Figure 7

The Mathematics of Life Insurance Design

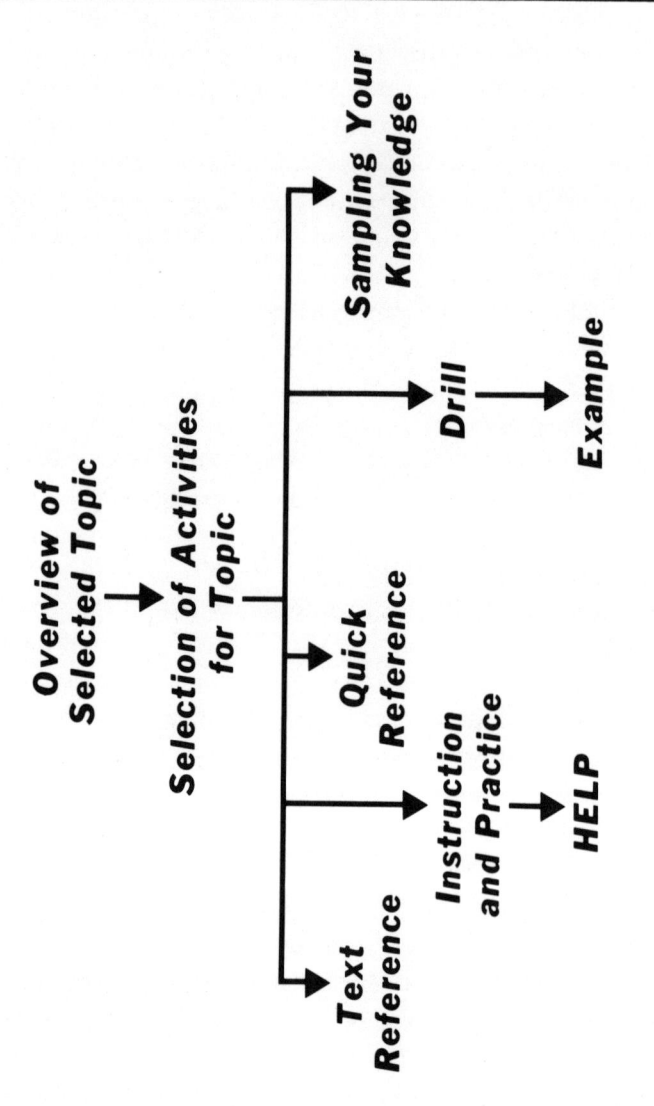

Design Format

As previously shown in Figure 4, this display provides the student with the main activity index for the subject-matter topic. This index provides the student with four or five instructional choices depending on the topic chosen—some topics do not lend themselves to drill—and is the point to which the student is always returned after completing one of the topic activities. "Text Reference" simply provides the student with a reference to the relevant pages of the course text covering the particular content area, as well as pointing out any additional non-text references for the topic. Another activity, Quick Reference, provides an on-line source of information concerning the content.

The student who chooses this activity will receive an index to a number of short instructional sequences similar to the one shown for Mortality Concepts in Figure 8. Note that the student is given the choice of seeing the short summary displays for an individual concept, an example of which appears in Figure 9, or seeing all the displays for the particular topic in their proper instructional sequence (option "h" on the index in Figure 8).

The third activity available to the student from the topic activity index is Sampling Your Knowledge, a ten-item test containing true/false and completion items covering the topic material. An illustrative Sampling Your Knowledge item from Mortality Concepts appears in Figure 10. Suppose the student has touched the touch-sensitive "TRUE" box on the screen display. The screen will flash that the statement is actually false, and why. Since 90 percent is the level of performance required for mastery of the ten-item quiz, PLATO immediately ends the test after the student has made a second error and gives him or her suggestions for remedial activities, as shown in Figure 11.

The Mathematics of Life Insurance program contains two instructional activities for each content topic where interaction with PLATO is designed to provide the basis for the

Figure 8

Quick Reference Index

Choose the letter of the concept you'd like: ▶

    a. Adjustments to Mortality Data

    b. How to Calculate the Probabilities of Death or Survival

    c. How to Read Data Shown on the 1958 CSO Mortality Table

    d. Important Factors in Designing a Mortality Table

    e. Life Expectancy

    f. Reasons Why Different Mortality Tables Are Used for Life Policies and and Annuity Contracts

    g. Types of Mortality Tables

    h. ALL OF THE ABOVE

Press SHIFT-NEXT to return to the Activities Index

From the Control Data PLATO® course, *The Mathematics of Life Insurance*, Copyright © 1978 by Control Data Corporation. Used by permission.

Design Format 45

Figure 9

Quick Reference Display

Reading Data Shown on the 1958 CSO Mortality Table --

````
----First 5 Years of 1958 CSO Table----
````

Age	Number living at beginning of designated year	Number dying during designated year
0	10,000,000	70,800
1	9,929,200	17,475
2	9,911,725	15,066
3	9,896,659	14,449
4	9,882,210	13,835
5	9,868,375	13,322

The <u>NUMBER LIVING</u> column shows the number living at the beginning of the year at each age. For example, the number living at the beginning of age 2 is 9,911,725.

Press NEXT to continue

From the Control Data PLATO® course, *The Mathematics of Life Insurance,* Copyright © 1978 by Control Data Corporation. Used by permission.

Figure 10

Test Item

The 1958 CSO Mortality Table includes an adjustment for graduation in order to ensure rates that are safe for all companies to use.

| TRUE | This statement is false. | FALSE |

The graduation adjustment is used to eliminate irregularities that may obscure the true characteristics of the population under observation.

| Touch here for the next question |

From the Control Data PLATO® course, *The Mathematics of Life Insurance,* Copyright © 1978 by Control Data Corporation. Used by permission.

Design Format

Figure 11

Feedback from Quiz

Oh no!!

Once again, you made more than one error.
Before retrying Sampling Your Knowledge,
we STRONGLY SUGGEST that you:
 1. Read Quick Reference or
        Text Reference; then
 2. Try some of the Drill problems.

 Press NEXT for Quick Reference; LAB for the
Text Reference, or BACK for the Activities Index.

From the Control Data PLATO® course, *The Mathematics of Life Insurance,* Copyright © 1978 by Control Data Corporation. Used by permission.

student's learning. The first activity, Instruction and Practice, provides the student with displays of text covering specific content areas and displays requiring the student to input an answer to a question posed on the screen. The student cannot move on to the next display without giving the correct answer to the question, but the lesson is programmed so that the student receives progressively broader hints on the display screen each time an incorrect answer is entered. This "prompting" continues until the student is finally told the correct answer after the third incorrect response. This prevents the student from ever becoming "stuck" at some point in the lesson with no way to continue in the instructional sequence, while requiring enough incorrect responses to discourage the student from "peeking" at the correct answer instead of actually working through the problem. As a further aid to students in solving Instruction and Practice exercises, the appropriate summary display from Quick Reference for the concept being tested is made available to the student any time he or she presses the HELP key on the keyboard. An example of an Instruction and Practice problem and the type of hint the student receives after an incorrect response appear in Figure 12.

The second interactive instructional activity provided for students in most of the content topics in *The Mathematics of Life Insurance* program is a randomly-generated series of Drill problems. This activity is designed so that the student can do as many or as few Drill problems as he or she desires in order to feel comfortable with the subject matter. The student always has the option to leave the drill exercises and return to the main activity index. The student is required to enter the correct answer for a particular drill exercise before moving on to another Drill problem. However, the student who enters an incorrect response receives the suggestion that he or she examine a sample solution to a similar problem (which can be accessed and displayed on the screen) before

Design Format 49

Figure 12

Practice Exercise

<pre>
                    HELP is available
</pre>

PRACTICE---Type in the word, words, or number which best
          completes each of the following statements.

In designing a mortality table, seven of the most
important factors to consider are:

  1. the   _population ok_   to be included in the survey;

  2. the type of > risk no   to be insured;

  3. the appropriate type of _____ ;

  4. classification of the data by _____ ;

  5. classification of the data by _____ ;

  6. effects of _____ ; and

  7. the period of _____ .

Think of life insurance policyowners vs. annuitants....

From the Control Data PLATO® course, *The Mathematics of Life Insurance,* Copyright © 1978 by Control Data Corporation. Used by permission.

attempting the problem again and is told the correct answer to the Drill problem after entering a third incorrect response. A sample Drill problem appears in Figure 13. Where mathematical calculations are required of the student in the interactive PLATO-based activities, a calculator that is activated by touching the lower right-hand corner of the display is provided for the student. However, while PLATO activities form the basis for instruction in the various content areas of *The Mathematics of Life Insurance* program, the PLATO lessons feature off-line references to textbooks, printed tables and readings, and audiotape/workbook review packages.

In addition to PLATO activities for 11 subject-matter areas, *The Mathematics of Life Insurance* also features a sample course examination which is made available to students who have mastered the Sampling Your Knowledge activities for each topic in the course. This is a very valuable learning experience for students who will be sitting for The American College's two-hour standardized examination, since PLATO can keep track of both how well they are pacing themselves and how high they are scoring in terms of the subject matter. Students receive feedback at both the half-way point in the examination and at the conclusion, reflecting both their pacing and their percentage score, and they are given suggestions for areas requiring remedial study at the conclusion of the examination. This activity differs somewhat from other PLATO instructional designs in that the student does not receive immediate feedback concerning the correctness of his or her response; since this activity was designed to simulate as closely as possible actual examination conditions, the student is not given feedback concerning the correctness of any individual response but rather is told subject-matter areas which seem to need remedial study.

The design of the course is flexible enough to allow individual students to tailor a program of activities which

Design Format

Figure 13

Drill Exercise

NEXT→more Drill   SHIFT-NEXT→leave Drill   HELP→examples

Use the 1958 CSO Mortality Table to answer the following questions. This table can be found on page 239 of Huebner & Black, or in your Supplemental Readings. Enter first the numerator, then the denominator, of your answer.

What is the probability that a person age 29 and a person age 33 will both survive another year?

Enter the correct operator (+,-,×,÷):

9480358 ok
————————————>
9500118 ok

From the Control Data PLATO® course, *The Mathematics of Life Insurance,* Copyright © 1978 by Control Data Corporation. Used by permission.

facilitate their learning styles yet provide enough structure to give students some guidance in their study efforts. Particular paths combining the different PLATO activities in specific sequences are suggested for students using the program for Introductory study, Supplemental study (in addition to attending a class, for example), and Review study in the introductory lesson for the course itself. Furthermore, a variety of recordkeeping features is built into the course so that the student can tell always which activities have been entered and/or completed; a sample display that a student might see approximately half-way through his or her course of study appears in Figure 14. Especially in the case of the adult learner, the PLATO student should be provided with sufficient guidance but always be allowed to make his or her own learning decisions and sequence his or her own individual course of study. Although the design of *The Mathematics of Life Insurance* was developed for a particular course, it is broadly applicable to a number of subject-matter areas and combines several PLATO-based instructional designs (simulation, drill, and tutorial, for example) discussed previously.

Acid-Base Titrations. The students studying chemical titrations on the PLATO system experience many of the same design formats as used in *The Mathematics of Life Insurance* material. Some of these design features are:
- introduction to the keyboard,
- table of contents,
- current status in the course,
- scores on completed sections,
- access to a calculator,
- assistance by pressing the HELP key,
- discussion of the topic,
- drill and practice,
- simulation/application of theory,
- use of random numbers in problems,
- review of exercise as many times as the student wishes,

Design Format 53

Figure 14

Progress Chart

TOPIC	SYK SCORES			SYK	I&P	DRILL	TR	QR
Probability*	100	0	0	*		*		+
Mortality*	100	90	0	*		*		+
Interest*	90	70	67	*	*		+	
Net Single Premiums*	100	70	0	*	*	*	+	+
Net Level Premiums*	90	50	0	*	-			+
Policy Reserves	80	70	40	-	-	*		+
Modified Reserves*	100	70	0	*	*	*	+	
Nonforfeiture Vals.	0	0	0				+	
Gross Premiums	0	0	0					
Surplus & Dividends	0	0	0					
Asset Share	0	0	0					

YOUR PROGRESS:

    SYK SCORES = your percentage scores for your last three attempts at Sampling Your Knowledge.
    SYK = Sampling Your Knowledge
    I&P = Instruction and Practice
    DRILL = Drill
    TR = Text Reference
    QR = Quick Reference

----

       * means that you have completed the activity
       - means that you have entered the activity
       + means that you have entered an activity
         which has no completion criterion

From the Control Data PLATO® course, *The Mathematics of Life Insurance,* Copyright © 1978 by Control Data Corporation. Used by permission.

- a note feature for communicating with the instructor, and
- specific response feedback.

One additional component of the *Acid-Base Titrations* material, which is essential in developing skills in chemical applications, is the analysis of data. A required part of this laboratory simulation is the successful collection of data followed by a correct analysis of the data.

The final step for this PLATO simulation is the submission of an experimental report by the student to the PLATO system. This report is graded immediately by the PLATO system. If improper data were collected, the student must repeat the simulated experiment. If the data were incorrectly analyzed, the student must re-analyze the data and then resubmit the report. The student must successfully complete the PLATO simulation before the actual laboratory experiment is initiated.

From the teacher's point of view, this PLATO simulation insures that the student understands the theory, application, and analysis of data before a laboratory experiment begins. Therefore, the time which the student spends in the laboratory is more productive. This reduces the expense of operating a laboratory and frees time for the student and teacher.

PLATO Learning Management

The design format of computer-managed instruction on PLATO is generic with respect to its flexibility in implementing diverse CMI courses. To examine the design format of PLATO learning management, we will look at the structure of curricula, modules, and instructional units. As stated earlier, the design consists of a curriculum which is composed of courses which are made up of modules, which in turn are composed of instructional units and a list of learning resources. Each instructional unit is composed of objectives, test items, and feedback.

Design Format 55

The curriculum is the largest block within PLATO learning management. A curriculum can be composed of up to 15 courses. A course may consist of up to 28 modules. Each module can contain from one to 30 objectives and from one to 1,800 test questions. In total, a single curriculum can consist of up to 12,600 objectives with over 750,000 associated test items. A very large instructional program, indeed.

Although the curriculum is the largest unit within PLATO learning management, it has little utility in and of itself other than for labeling and identification purposes. More important are courses, which are constructed from individual modules. Courses consist of individual modules selected by the instructor from those prepared by an author. Within a course, up to seven individual strategies may be prescribed for student use. Each student, however, would be assigned one strategy. Figure 15 illustrates the concept of alternate instructional strategies for a course. Assume that a history course has been constructed of five modules, A, B, C, D, and E, with the respective time periods covered by these modules. Strategy one illustrates a linear approach in which a student would be required to study in a given, prescribed order. In strategy two, the first module to be taken is specified, but the student has the choice of studying either B or C before proceeding with D and E. In strategy three, another approach to sequencing is illustrated. Based upon either student choice or instructor mandate, students could be assigned to one of the three strategies.

This example is small and simple, but in microcosm it illustrates how courses in general can be organized to produce a flexible and responsive learning environment. Expanding slightly on the example, entire history courses could be organized in sequences which would emphasize chronology, geography, or combinations of these approaches. The instructor has the option of providing the student with as much, or

Figure 15

Course Alternatives

A	U.S.	1770-1800
B	U.S. North	1800-1860
C	U.S. South	1800-1860
D	U.S.	1860-1900
E	England-U.S.	1800-1900

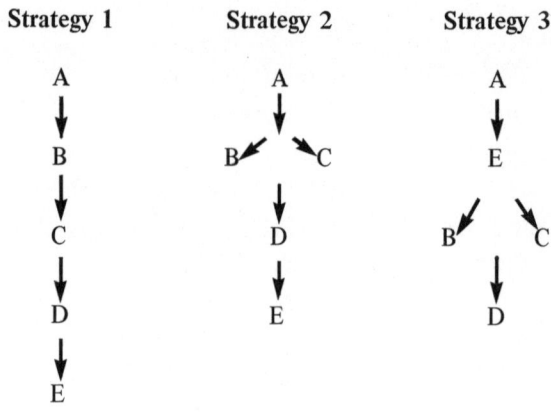

Design Format

as little, flexibility in sequencing his or her learning as is deemed desirable. For purposes of curriculum research, the flexibility, combined with PLATO's recordkeeping, is powerful.

It has been seen from earlier illustrations that the module is an important building block in PLATO learning management. The module contains information necessary to generate student tests. It can have an introduction which provides a student with a brief overview of the module content, the number of questions in the test, and the level of performance required to master the test. Another module description, which is not accessible to the student, provides other authors and instructors with specific information regarding content and intended use of the module.

To implement the variable management strategy, an instructor has the following options:
- displaying requirements for module mastery;
- allowing the student to waive the pretest;
- showing a mastery or nonmastery feedback message;
- stopping a test before all objectives have been tested because of exceptionally good or poor student performance; and
- testing on only previously unmastered objectives.

Instructional units consisting of objectives and associated test items are the smallest building blocks within PLATO learning management and are the heart of the building process. Students are provided with test items for each objective and, depending upon the results of the test, receive a prescription of learning resources. Test items may be generated using one of the standard PLATO learning management designs, or specialized test formats may be generated by the author.

To facilitate the variable management strategy, at the instructional unit level, the instructor has the option to:
- display the objective before showing the associated questions;

- show for each objective before testing the number of test questions to be presented and the score necessary to achieve mastery;
- interrupt and terminate a test before all questions scheduled have been answered because of exceptionally good or poor student performance;
- inform the student following testing of each objective how well he or she did; and
- show either a specifically written mastery or nonmastery message at the conclusion of testing for an objective.

Two substructures flow from the results of testing in each instructional unit: the study prescription and the gradebook. When a student has completed a test, PLATO learning management selects or helps the student select learning resources that are designed to bring the student to mastery level on the unmastered objectives. The list of learning resources chosen is called a study prescription. At an instructor's option, the student may participate in selecting learning resources or may receive automatically generated prescriptions.

The PLATO learning management gradebook records individual student performance data as well as group or class data. Depending upon the privileges of the user referencing the gradebook, all or part of the information contained in the gradebook may be inspected or changed. Authors can see a wide variety of information for each module, each instructional unit, and each question. Likewise, the instructors can access a wide variety of data for individual students and for a class as a whole. Students can access information on their own performance.

PLATO Learning Management Examples

In the United Airlines Flight Operations Training course, there are 28 modules made up of 100 instructional units including over 2,500 test items. This structure allows students, instructors, and authors to monitor student progress and overall performance of the training program.

The *Research Methods* course of The American College is composed of ten modules made up of 61 instructional units including approximately 110 questions. Because of the developmental nature of this course, items are frequently added or deleted.

Summary

It can be seen that the design format of PLATO is very flexible. PLATO learning management offers a standardized, yet flexible, format within which an author can develop material. To use this format, the author need know very little about computer programming. However, for an author who knows the TUTOR language, the design formats which can be developed are virtually unlimited.

IV.

OUTCOMES

The most important outcomes of PLATO accrue to the student, but authors and instructors also benefit.

Student

The most significant outcome of the PLATO instructional design is the individualization of education. In addition, the design facilitates a confidential relationship with students and facilitates recordkeeping. Finally, the computing system facilitates simulations.

Individualization is significant economically. Through an individualized education program, it is possible to have a student work on appropriate material and *only* appropriate material until he or she has mastered objectives. Students often come into a learning situation already having mastered a number of the objectives to be covered during the learning session. By enabling students to test out of portions of the curriculum and demonstrate their mastery of objectives without having to go through the learning materials, an economy of time is attained. This economy is extremely important in business, where the cost of education and training is high, both in terms of the cost of the training itself and in terms of the cost of the salaries of persons being trained.

Individualization of education has two aspects; first, the individualization of the objectives a student pursues; and, second, the individualization of the teaching/learning strategy used.

Individualization can imply different objectives for different students. Rather than require all students to study the same objectives, students can study objectives that meet their specific needs. PLATO facilitates the tailoring of educational programs to individual needs.

Individualization of education can also take place through the use of alternate teaching/learning strategies. Alternatives for implementing strategies may include: the sequence of objectives; amounts of repetition, review, motivational materials, and drill and practice; and the degree of student control.

The individualization of instruction can be under student control, under instructor control, or some combination of the two. Many students, and particularly adults, like to move through instructional materials at a pace and following a strategy of their own choosing. PLATO facilitates this student initiative. On the other hand, it may be desirable for the instructor to dictate the instructional strategy to be followed by a student. Some students feel that the teacher knows best, and they desire strong direction.

An additional outcome of this instructional design is the simulation of real-world situations. Simulation can be a powerful learning tool, while at the same time providing a bridge between "textbook learning" and real-world events. Real situations which may be time-consuming, dangerous, or costly can be simulated effectively on PLATO. PLATO's graphics capability is of significant benefit in producing this outcome.

Flexibility in scheduling assists in meeting student needs. Class time and location are not as restrictive as they are in many other types of instruction. Since most PLATO systems run at least 16 hours per day, students may study at a time of their own choosing. All courses are available at any time of the day, so a student is not restricted by a specific hourly schedule for instruction. Geographic flexibility is also highly desirable in bringing instruction to students where they need it.

For example, students may use the Control Data PLATO Network at any one of hundreds of sites throughout the United States and around the world. There is, of course, the restriction that a terminal must be available at a geographic location for students to use. Geographic flexibility is especially important for large corporations with employees in locations throughout the world. Bringing employees into a central location for education and training can be extremely expensive, both in terms of direct travel costs and, more importantly, in terms of loss of productivity during the time of travel.

Confidentiality of the student-instructor relationship can be maintained through the PLATO system. Although the popular conception of a computer is as an impersonal machine, students using computer-based instruction often cite personalization and confidentiality as desirable characteristics of their interaction. Students who have not had positive learning experiences are often "turned on" by the positive, patient thrust of computer-based education. These students develop a trust in the confidential relationship they develop with PLATO and are able to make progress they had not thought possible. Although the instructor does have access to student files, the student is able to practice, to make mistakes, and to learn without exposing himself or herself to peer review.

Management of student work is facilitated through the recordkeeping system of PLATO. The system can maintain a record of student activity and provide that record to the student on demand. The system can also maintain a record of student progress and return the student to the appropriate place in the program if a break is taken. The recordkeeping system is also valuable as a motivational tool. Students can usually see the progress they are making in their study.

Author

The PLATO system can be used as a tool by instructional developers. Curriculum materials can be entered directly into the computing system at a terminal. Once the materials are entered, they may be edited, revised, and tested using the system. More detail on the developmental aspects of PLATO will be provided in the next chapter.

The author may also monitor student progress in a course for the purpose of developing data which can be used for future course improvement. Data which are available to the author include performance scores for each activity, time spent, completing status and position in the curriculum, correct and incorrect responses, and requests for assistance. These data are highly useful in developing a truly experience-based education program which is responsive to students' needs.

PLATO's on-line consultants enable an author to receive assistance in curriculum development and in programming. The PLATO learning management system provides structure within which authors may develop courses and curricula.

Instructor

The flexibility of time and geography, as well as the recordkeeping capability of PLATO, are very useful for the teacher. Students may be signed into a course and use it for many hours a day and at a wide variety of locations. Within a specific geographic location, this feature provides a great deal of time flexibility and, combined with the geographic flexibility, provides considerable assistance to the administrator in scheduling education and training.

The recordkeeping capability of PLATO is useful to the instructor. The instructor can access data through a PLATO terminal. The data would include, but not be limited to, items such as (a) the names of students actually registered for a course, (b) the number of modules completed by each individual student and by the class as a whole, (c) the level of student performance on material with respect to an individual student as well as a class as a whole, and (d) the amount of time spent on individual modules with respect to individual students and a class as a whole.

Examples of Outcomes

With the general outcomes described above for student, author, and instructor, let us now outline more specific outcomes through the sample programs that have been illustrated in this book.

The Mathematics of Life Insurance

The most basic outcome for students using *The Mathematics of Life Insurance* PLATO lesson is the participation in individualized, interactive learning experiences. In most of the PLATO learning activities, the student receives immediate feedback for an incorrect response and is provided specific guidance as to how to remedy that learning deficiency. And, rather than having a single learning activity, reading a text, available to him or her for each subject-matter area, *The Mathematics of Life Insurance* student has a choice of interactive learning activities.

For students such as The American College's CLU students, busy professional adults who study part-time in addition to maintaining a full professional schedule, *The Mathematics of Life Insurance* PLATO course offers significant advantages in increased flexibility in scheduling learning sessions around students' work schedules. Each student has his or her own set of personal PLATO records maintained from session to session, enabling the student to return to work at exactly the point at which he or she ended previously.

Furthermore, interaction with PLATO activities can significantly reduce students' anxiety in testing situations. The interaction required by PLATO helps the student to feel comfortable making an overt response using information that he or she has studied, and an activity such as the Sample CLU Examination can simulate examination conditions without the anxiety and pressure associated with the real situation.

The result of students using PLATO for instructors and developers is the generation of a body of student performance data that can be used to revise the PLATO lessons to make them more effective. Furthermore, for The American College with its 60,000 active students across the United States, the Control Data PLATO Network with learning centers in major cities makes it possible to distribute interactive PLATO-based materials to a national student population.

Acid-Base Titrations

The general outcomes discussed as well as those mentioned in *The Mathematics of Life Insurance* apply to the chemistry course. The simulation of laboratory exercises is an efficient and safe means of preparing students for actual laboratory work. The flexibility of allowing students to study evenings at locations such as the library and in residence halls provides additional flexibility within which students can schedule their study.

PLATO Learning Management

The general outcomes already mentioned for PLATO, that is, individualization of education, confidentiality, and record-keeping, hold for the CMI instructional design contained within PLATO. Using PLATO learning management, students receive programs of study based upon their individual needs. This can be accomplished through the use of a variable management strategy within a curriculum and through the building of alternate curricula for existing modules. Students' learning strategies can be varied through selection of alternate materials referenced in instructional units. The scheduling of students and the time flexibility allowable through PLATO are facilitated by its recordkeeping capability.

Authors and instructors derive benefits from this design. PLATO learning management provides a design format within which authors can construct and evaluate courses. A likely, although not primary, outcome is the fostering of good curriculum development practices by authors.

Instructors and other administrators benefit from the "cafeteria" of modules which can be used to develop courses and curriculum, and they can effectively monitor student progress in mastering the curriculum.

At United Airlines, one outcome of their CMI effort has been to significantly reduce the time required for training, while at the same time maintaining the degree of excellence expected from the program. A conventional program would normally take four weeks, while the average time for the first 367 pilots completing the program was 9.6 days. In terms of productive capacity of flight crews, the economic value of the time-saving is obvious.

The outcome of the developmental work on the course in *Research Methods* at The American College will be a tested educational program which can be utilized as PLATO learning management or with modifications in noncomputer-based individualized education designs.

V.
DEVELOPMENTAL GUIDE

The focus of this chapter is upon the developmental aspects of PLATO as related to the course author. The principles discussed in this chapter apply to the development process, irrespective of whether the author is an individual or a team. The authors of this book firmly believe that higher quality programs can be produced more efficiently through the use of developmental teams as contrasted with courses developed by a sole author.

The development process will be treated in four sections: (1) planning, (2) design, (3) development, and (4) testing. Much of the activity involved in the development of good computer-based educational materials is the same as the activity involved in the systematic development of materials in any media. The need for the course or materials must be established prior to other planning activity. Instructional objectives, objectives-based test items, and learning resources must be identified or developed. PLATO's significant contribution to the effort is to act as a facilitator of the development effort, especially in the writing and testing phases.

Planning

The planning which takes place in the development of

computer-based educational materials is not unlike the planning which does or should take place in the development of any educational material. Assuming that the need for the materials has been established, the author considers the general objectives, the student population to be using the program, the environment in which the program will be used, and the expected useful life of the program. Developing course objectives is an obvious early step in the design of any good educational program, as is the specification of the student population to be receiving the program. Because of the wide variety of uses of PLATO, it is important to take into account the environment in which the PLATO terminal will deliver instruction. It is often desirable to include in your planning materials other than the PLATO terminal; for example, to use laboratory simulation or to use other media. In planning a PLATO learning management course, the consideration of nonPLATO instructional resources may be paramount.

In addition to the presentation of content and subject matter, course design should also take into account the diagnosis of student difficulty, strategies for accommodating individual differences, feedback to students, and recordkeeping. The PLATO system facilitates each of these.

Design

The line of demarcation between planning and design is not a clear one, since detailed planning can aid and shorten the development process. On the other hand, the development of PLATO courses is not a linear process; early writing and testing may cause the author to re-think the original design.

The first half of the design process involves deciding on the specific instructional designs that will be used or combined to form the total PLATO learning environment for the student. This process involves careful consideration of the way in

Developmental Guide

which the designs discussed in the Design Format chapter of this volume, as well as combinations of these designs, can be applied to the specific subject matter that the author wishes to teach. In some situations, it will be relatively straightforward to choose a design; for example, if one wished to teach a process, a representative design line flow of current through an electronic circuit might be most appropriate. But if the process was one with which the student would be interacting, a simulation lesson, i.e., a chemistry experiment, might be more effective. For the novice designer of PLATO lessons, it can be very valuable to spend some time at a PLATO terminal looking at demonstration lessons of courses that other authors have designed. This will give one a feeling for the range of instructional designs that can be implemented on PLATO and provide ideas for one's own lessons.

The second part of the design phase involves the actual design of the lesson to be programmed and delivered via PLATO. It is important to differentiate between design and programming because these are two separate processes. The designer need not know TUTOR, the PLATO programming language. He or she should know the range of capabilities of PLATO, however, in order to design lessons that make the best of PLATO's unique resources. First, one should identify the various components of each lesson and decide how the components should be connected to one another, and in a broader sense how the several lessons in a curriculum might be connected to one another. Students may move through a PLATO lesson in a strictly linear manner; they can be given the opportunity to choose to review a section before proceeding onward; they can be given the opportunity to branch-off in directions of their own choosing; or they can be provided an instructional sequence based on their individual prior responses to earlier questions presented by PLATO. All such instructional decisions should be set out on at least a working basis before proceeding further in the design of the lessons.

At this point in the design process, the designer should apply the chosen instructional design and the instructional decisions made for the particular course to the development of a programming script that the developer can use to generate the required program code to deliver the instructional design via PLATO. There are four basic components of a PLATO "frame": display (text and graphics), response judging/feedback, routing or branching, and recordkeeping. The designer must tell the developer what words of text, tables, or graphic images he or she wishes to have appearing on the screen, when, and in what sequence. Because of PLATO's animation capabilities, this is not unlike scripting an animated film. The designer must also tell the developer what questions to ask the student, what the correct responses might be, incorrect responses that might be anticipated on the basis of commonly-made errors, and feedback to be provided to the student in the case of both anticipated and unanticipated errors. The designer must tell the developer where the student is to be taken after completing a particular frame or instructional unit, and, if this is conditional on the student's responses, what the conditions are. This branching can be under the control of the student through specific control keys located on PLATO's keyboard or can be handled by PLATO based on "flags" or "counters" that were set when the student made particular responses. And, finally, the designer should tell the developer what data should be collected on the student's performance, what parts of this should be made available to the student so that he or she can track his or her own progress, and what parts should be returned to the designer for use in evaluating and revising the PLATO lessons.

An example of the design script that was used as part of the Interest lessons for *The Mathematics of Life Insurance* is shown in Figure 16. While this script was written with the capabilities of PLATO in mind, the designer did not know

Developmental Guide 73

Figure 16

Design Script

FINAL COPY
Interest Concepts

Write:

Practice—What is the accumulated value of a 3-year annuity due of $2 at 4½% interest?

Program Note: Place $2 over A, B, and C of the diagram.

ANSWER: 6.5540 or $6.55 or $6.56
 If the student answers correctly, write "Good!"
 If the student answers incorrectly, write:
  Find the product of:
  3.27820 the accumulated value of an annuity due of $1 for 3 years at 4½% interest
  x $2   the payment each year

Program Note: Erase from "What is the . . .?" on, plus the values in the diagram. If the student answers the above question correctly on the FIRST TRY, bypass the enclosed block below; otherwise:

Write:

Practice—What is the accumulated value of a 3-year annuity due of $3 at 2½% interest?

Program Note: Place $3 over A, B, and C of the diagram.

ANSWER: 9.45753 or $9.46
 If the student answers correctly, write "Good!"
 If the student answers 9.83460 or $9.83, write:
   "Use 2½% interest."
 If the student gives any other incorrect answer, write:
   Find the product of:
   3.15251 the accumulated value of an annuity due of $1 for 3 years at 2½% interest
   x $3   the payment each year

---

the specific program-language code that would be required to execute the design. An additional advantage of a nonPLATO-based design script is that it fosters easy implementation on other computer-based education systems besides PLATO, if the need for such implementation ever arises.

Development

This is the process by which the designer's ideas are applied to the generation of a program code that will execute the chosen instructional design via PLATO. In developing a program code, the author can use two different modes of operation. In one, the author can enter material as he or she would use a normal typewriter and allow the PLATO system itself to generate the appropriate program code when the display is looking just the way the developer wants it; this is known as "ID" (Insert Display) mode and works primarily for the display and text portions of the lessons. Except for PLATO learning management, the author will still have to generate some TUTOR program-language code to complete the development of the lesson. This mode of operation is in contrast to writing lesson material directly in TUTOR, a mode that is less amenable to seeing how the lesson will appear to the student. It is likely that an author will alternate between these two modes, depending on the material being developed and the ease of utilizing a particular mode of operation. In team development efforts, a differentiation of staff function according to the individual's proficiency in TUTOR may be advantageous.

Although a detailed discussion of the TUTOR programming language is beyond the scope of this volume, there are a number of general considerations that should be kept in mind during the development of the display, response judging, branching, and recordkeeping portions of a PLATO lesson.

The PLATO display screen is 64 normal characters wide by 32 lines, with standard characters appearing on the screen at

Developmental Guide

a rate of 180 characters per second. Since information appears on the screen character-by-character, avoid having too much of a display appear on the screen at once. The student's natural tendency will be to try to read the material as it appears, and this will quickly become tiring when long displays are presented. Furthermore, one should not have too much information on the screen at any one time, since large borders make screen displays easier to read. Highlights, underlines, spacing, and animation can be used to organize and feature information on the display, but remember that any such device quickly loses its impact if it is over-used. In addition to keeping these display techniques in mind, the developer should be sure to tell the student via the display screen which control or branching keys are active; for example, "Press BACK to Review this Segment," "Press HELP for an Example," etc.

The PLATO system has an on-line, interactive display editor available to all authors. This editor allows for the input of text, the sizing and rotation of text, generation of line drawings, and location of response cues. In addition to these features, the author can reposition a portion or an entire display, center text, and specify margins and justify text. With these editing features, the author's ideas can be quickly and easily transformed into completed displays on the PLATO system.

Response judging and feedback are perhaps the most complicated parts of programming PLATO, because PLATO offers such flexibility in this area that a developer requires a good working knowledge of TUTOR to make the best use of all of PLATO's judging features. Because of the on-line reference sources, however, it does not take a novice developer long to become proficient in this area of programming.

Careful response judging is crucial to PLATO, because it can quickly lose its credibility as an instructional medium if

it either judges a response that the student knows to be right as wrong, or if it judges a known wrong response to be correct. Therefore, one should take care to program the judging for a particular response to take into consideration:
- synonyms (for both correct and anticipated incorrect responses);
- alternate forms of the same answer (for example, 4.5 vs. 4½);
- extra words that may be included in the student's response but which may be ignored for judging purposes;
- numerical tolerance (to allow for rounding error in calculations);
- misspellings or poor typing (PLATO can be programmed to accept a response as correct if the spelling is close enough to be recognizable, and this should be used except where spelling is a crucial part of the skill being tested);
- gross visual and touch discriminations if the touch-sensitive feature is being employed; and
- extraneous responses that can be ignored if the student is choosing his or her responses from a predetermined set of keys (as in the case of a multiple-choice test item) or screen touch locations.

Students should be given feedback for correct responses as well as incorrect responses; such feedback can be motivational or can be used to elaborate upon the original question. Specific feedback should be included for anticipated wrong responses so that the student will know exactly what it is that he or she is doing wrong in solving the problem. In addition, a broad "catch-all" hint should be programmed so that the student is given some idea of how to answer the question, even if the specific error being made cannot be identified. Both of these types of feedback can be conditional, depending on the value of various counters, such as the number of times that the student has attempted to answer the particular question. This makes it possible for one to program a specific hint to appear after one or two incorrect responses, with the correct answer being displayed after a third incorrect response. Feedback for incorrect responses can take the form of suggestions of how to solve the problem being asked, remedial sequences that can be accessed before attempting the question again, or off-line references such as appropriate texts.

Routing and branching refer to the student's movement from one instructional situation to the next within the PLATO lesson. This can be handled by PLATO, based on the student's responses, or can be under the control of the student. Adult learners seem to respond more positively to being given an index of learning activities and being allowed to choose whatever activities they like. However, a high percentage of the time they choose the sequence indicated on the index, so the designers can use this device to provide guidance for students. Wherever appropriate, "HELP sequences" (as they are called on PLATO, since students initiate them by pressing the "HELP" key on the keyboard) should be provided so the student can quickly review relevant concepts, rules, or examples and then return to the point of the lesson where he or she was prior to requesting HELP.

It is important to program recordkeeping into one's lessons for several reasons. It allows PLATO to keep track of the student's progress, so that it can "hold the student's place" in the lesson between learning sessions, and it also allows the student to assess his or her own progress, something that can be quite motivational to the student. However, recordkeeping is perhaps even more vital in that instructors can track their students' progress through PLATO materials by quickly examining the students' records.

There are a number of features of the PLATO system itself which provide assistance to authors. There is an "Aids" package which enables the author to be prompted in how to use the system more effectively. A group of consultants uses the Control Data PLATO Network so that it is possible for an author to obtain on-line assistance in the development of materials. In addition, an author may consult with other authors using the communications features of the system.

Testing

Once materials have been developed, they may be tested using the PLATO system. Three types of testing are highly recommended. These are tests by the author, tests by a subject-matter expert, and tests by actual students.

The author will need to test the material to be sure that the material is operating in a manner that the planning had prescribed. The flow of material, including the various paths that a student might follow, needs to be checked in detail. Mechanical checks for errors in program code syntax can be performed by the computer itself; however, it is important that the author carefully check out the logic of each lesson. The author also will need to check the various screen displays to see that they are both correct and visually satisfying. It is also important at this point that the author check to see that "cute" material has not become excessive. Let us explain this point in greater detail.

Because of the excellent graphics capability of PLATO and because of the ease of copying material from one display to another, it is tempting for an author to create a clever graphic and then use it repetitively to a degree which annoys the student. This is particularly true of graphics which are slow in appearing on the screen and, thus, the students must wait over again for the "clever" material to be displayed. Often in the heat of developmental efforts such cute graphics would appear to be appropriate. However, when viewed in the context of a total lesson, they can become overwhelming. It is only by a complete check of the total course by the author that such an appropriate or inappropriate technique may be discovered before students use the material.

A separate subject-matter check of the material should be carried out even if the subject-matter expert and the author are one and the same person. It is not possible for an author to pay close attention to two aspects of an instructional program at the same time. While the author is acting as subject-matter expert in checking out the program, it is difficult, if not impossible, to anticipate the various system capabilities and operations and to pay attention to those as well.

The instructional program then should be tested using one or more students. It is desirable to do some testing in the presence of the author. Although PLATO has a significant recordkeeping ability, additional information can be obtained by watching a student proceed through the subject matter. Ideally, the author would devote full attention to watching a student proceed through the subject matter and would make notes on his or her progress. However, it is sometimes economically more desirable for the author to pursue some other activity simultaneously.

The material should be tested not only in a laboratory environment, but also in a real-world or production environment. That is, if students would be using the lesson at a remote site, care should be taken to test the materials at least on a limited basis using the remote site in the manner in which the materials will routinely be used. If a student is required to go to a learning center, sign up for a course, assemble a variety of audio-visual materials to use in conjunction with PLATO, and then work through the materials, it would be desirable to have a student attempt to do this as part of the developmental testing. The logistical testing of a program can be critical in insuring its success.

The type of student used in the testing procedure is important. In general, students used in the testing sample should be representative of those who will be in the group finally using the study materials. It is desirable to have students who are "bright" and also some who are "slow" test out the materials. If a wide range of reading levels is anticipated in the students who will eventually take the program, it would be desirable to test out the material with students having high reading ability as well as with those having a low reading ability. It is not necessary to have a large number of students participate in the early try-out of materials. Often three or four students are sufficient.

During the initial testing process and during production and use of a course, the "comments" feature of PLATO is a valuable tool. As a student is working through the instructional material, he or she may very simply indicate to the computer that he or she wishes to make a comment on the material. The computer then interrupts the normal instructional program and allows the student to type in a comment. While the student is typing in a comment, the material he or she has been working on remains on the screen. Thus, if a student is uncertain about a particular aspect of material displayed on the screen, he or she can refer to it in typing the comment. After finishing the comment, the student returns to the normal flow of the program. The comments are stored for the author, and the recordkeeping procedure indicates to the author not only what the comment is, but also who made the comment and specifically the exact portion of the lesson to which the comment relates. With this information, the author can either correct the program if an error has been made, or, if desirable, can communicate back to the student directly via PLATO to clarify points that have been misunderstood. This latter aspect of PLATO introduces a highly personal component to what has sometimes been thought to be an impersonal, mechanical device.

Examples of Development

With the developmental considerations previously described in mind, more specific suggestions for development will be discussed. Extensive use is made of figures in order to provide models for development.

The Mathematics of Life Insurance

Figure 16 presented a page from the design script used in *The Mathematics of Life Insurance* lessons from the Instruction and Practice for Interest Concepts. Note that it contains information to be presented on the display screen, the correct answer (including allowable numerical tolerance to reflect the possibility of rounding errors during the computation of the response), feedback to be presented after an incorrect response, and an additional problem to be presented if the student did not answer the first one on the first try.

Figure 17 presents the TUTOR code required to generate that design; lines 268 through 301 reflect the problem presented at the top of Figure 16, while the additional problem presented in the box on Figure 16 begins at line 302. This is presented in no way to intimidate the reader, since TUTOR is just as much a "foreign" language as French might be to someone who had no knowledge of it. Rather, it was included to illustrate the benefits of designing one's lessons in a script-type format similar to Figure 16. It is much easier to visualize one's design in a script that does not get involved in program code; the design can then be turned over to a developer for execution in TUTOR.

Figure 18 shows what the instructional sequence presented in design form in Figure 16 and in program code form in Figure 17 would look like to a student, sitting at a PLATO terminal, who has just entered an unanticipated, incorrect response.

Figure 17

TUTOR Code

268	unit	ininstc
269	help	ad
270	do	helpis
271	do	return
272	do	avadtitl
273	at	2003
274	write	PRACTICE—What is the accumulated value of a 3-year
275		annuity due of $2 at 4.5% interest?
276	at	1718
277	do	abcd
278	at	1718
279	write	$2 $2 $2
280	mode	write
281	draw	2135;2146
282	arrow	2134
283	long	9
284	do	calcset
285	join	calcdo
286	putd	/$//
287	specs	
288	ansv	6.55,.01
289	if	ntries=1
290	.	at 2150
291	.	write Good!
292	.	calc blowit=1
293	endif	
294	no	
295	do	wrong
296	at	2303
297	writec	ntries=3, The correct answer is $6.56,Find the product of:
298		3.27820 the accum. value of a 4.5% ann. due of $1 for 3 yrs.
299		x $2 the payment each year,,
300	endarrow	
301	branch	blowit=1,1nomore,x
302	do	calcnext
303	mode	rewrite
304	at	2003
305	write	PRACTICE—What is the accumulated value of a 3-year
306		annuity due of $3 at 2.5% interest?
307	at	1703
308	write	$3 $3 $3
309	at	1718
310	do	abcd
311	mode	write
312	draw	2135;2146
313	arrow	2134

Developmental Guide

Figure 18

Student Display

HELP is available

Rate of Interest	Year	Compound Interest Values			
		Accumulated Value of $1	Present Value of $1	Accumulated Value of an Annuity Due of $1	Present Value of an Annuity Due of $1
4.5%	1	1.04500	.95694	1.04500	1.00000
	2	1.09203	.91573	2.13703	1.95694
	3	1.14117	.87630	3.27820	2.87267
2.5%	1	1.02500	.97561	1.02500	1.00000
	2	1.05062	.95181	2.07562	1.97651
	3	1.07689	.92860	3.15251	2.92742

CALCULATING THE ACCUMULATED VALUE OF AN ANNUITY DUE:

$$\frac{\$2}{A} \quad \frac{\$2}{B} \quad \frac{\$2}{C} \quad \frac{}{D}$$

PRACTICE--What is the accumulated value of a 3-year annuity due of $2 at 4.5% interest? > 1.09 no

Find the product of:
3.27820   the accum. value of a 4.5% ann. due of $1 for 3 yrs.
× $2   the payment each year

[Calculator]   on [OFF]

From the Control Data PLATO® course, *The Mathematics of Life Insurance,* Copyright © 1978 by Control Data Corporation. Used by permission.

PLATO Learning Management

The development of materials in the PLATO learning management format has many factors in common with the development of PLATO materials in general. The significant difference is that the CMI design is highly structured so that the author can develop materials without knowing TUTOR. It is possible to use CAI material written in the TUTOR language within a PLATO learning management lesson. However, it is not necessary.

PLATO learning management provides a detailed structure for the development of lessons. Figures 19, 20, and 21 illustrate the general structure available to assist authors in developing materials. While it is not feasible in this book to go into detail with respect to the function of each of the prompts, a few will be used as illustrations.

For each module, a PLATO generated display provides information of the several aspects of the module. A display from the *Research Methods* course is shown in Figure 19. By typing in the appropriate number, the author may see additional detail and edit the material. When changes are made, this summary display is automatically updated.

The line numbered 2 (in Figure 19) indicates the number of Instructional Units that have been entered into the module. In this case, two have been entered. If the author calls for additional detail by entering the number 2, the display shown in Figure 20 can be obtained. This display is again generated by PLATO and reflects the status of several aspects of the IU. It can be noted in the figure that the objective for the IU is stated, the objective can be classified according to Bloom's Taxonomy, as is seen in 3, and information is given concerning the testing strategy and feedback. By entering "4," specific questions can be accessed and edited. Figure 21 illustrates one question for the IU. To modify the text of the item or to modify any of the associated specifications does not require knowledge of

Figure 19

Module Overview

PLATO learning management

1. <u>Title:</u> Sampling
   (module file = resm5)

2. <u>IUs/Questions</u>
   (2 IUs entered)

3. <u>Lesson used as a test</u>
   (option not in use)

4. <u>Learning Resources</u>
   (2 LRs entered)

5. <u>Testing Strategy</u>
   Sequentially measure
   all objectives.

6. <u>Scoring Procedure</u>
   Module Mastery is assigned
   when student masters 80%
   of the IUs in the test.

---

7. Student Introduction: entered
8. Mastery Feedback: entered
9. Non-Mastery Feedback: entered

Module Space Used =
656 of 1920 words

Enter item number.

LAB for Verification (now verified for on-line testing)

SHIFT-DATA for Directory   COPY to take test

From the Control Data PLATO® course, *Research Methods,* Copyright © 1980 by Control Data Corporation. Used by permission.

Figure 20

Instructional Unit Overview

```
1   IU # 1 of 2:  5.1                           MODULE:   resm5
2                   ▓▓▓ OBJECTIVE ▓▓▓
    ┌─────────────────────────────────────────────────────────┐
    │ to describe the basic nature of sampling, including the │
    │ basic concepts, the rationale for sampling, and the     │
    │ validity of a sample                                    │
    └─────────────────────────────────────────────────────────┘


3   CLASSIFICATION              ✓ Unclassified
       Knowledge           Comprehension    Application        Analysis
       Synthesis           Evaluation


                                              ┌──────────────────────────────┐
                                              │                      ENTERED │
4   QUESTIONS    ( 3 entered)                 │ 5 TESTING STRATEGY       yes │
                                              │ 6 SCORING PROCEDURE  default │
                                              │                              │
                                              │ 7 MASTERY FEEDBACK        no │
                                              │ 8 NON-MASTERY FEEDBACK    no │
                                              └──────────────────────────────┘


         Enter line number.

         LAB to add an IU after this one
         SHIFT-NEXT to display IU 2
```

From the Control Data PLATO® course, *Research Methods,* Copyright © 1980 by Control Data Corporation. Used by permission.

Figure 21

Test Question Overview

```
 ┌ QUESTION: 5.1.1      IU: 5.1            MODULE: resm5
 P  POINTS: Mastered=  1, Not Mastered=  0   TYPE: Mult. Choice
 1 All of the following statements concerning statistical
 2 terminology are correct EXCEPT:
 3
 4     a) A population is the total collection of elements
 5        about which a researcher wishes to make inferences.
 6     b) An element is the subject on which a researcher takes
 7        a measurement.
 8     c) A statistic is an estimate of a population value.
 9     d) A parameter is an estimate of a statistic.
```

L	Limit =	1 choice
J	Judging =	whole
S	Scoring =	match
C	Criterion=	match

1	a	✔
2	b	✔
3	c	✔
4	d	✔

Type an option letter or answer number to change.
BACK when finished.   SHIFT-HELP to abort changes.

| T | TEXT | G | GRAPHICS | F | FEEDBACK: None Entered |

From the Control Data PLATO® course, *Research Methods,* Copyright © 1980 by Control Data Corporation. Used by permission.

TUTOR. All modifications are made by typing in text or by other key presses as prompted. The structure with its inherent prompting, recordkeeping, and editing is ideal for developing and evaluating instructional material irrespective of whether the end-product is to be in a computer-managed format or in print.

Other Aids to Development

The authors have used an additional planning document developed by their colleague, Lillian G. Pedrick, in preparing to develop PLATO learning management materials. The document is shown in Figure 22. With the worksheet, an author can plan and document the relationship between objectives and test items, text references, workbook learning activities, and PLATO learning activities. Two other worthwhile features of PLATO provide assistance to the author. A PLATO lesson called "PLMAIDS" describes in considerable detail the features of PLATO learning management. For a new author, this lesson provides an introduction.

The second important lesson for CMI authors is "PLM-NOTES." This lesson is a note file through which individual authors can communicate with Control Data Corporation experts in order to solve difficult problems or discuss potential improvements. It is interesting to note that PLATO learning management is a dynamic system, and the historical record of suggestions and comments by users was a precursor of improvements that have been made. The lesson also permits the exchange of information between authors. This feature is extremely beneficial in promoting the feeling and reality of a community of authors as contrasted with authors in isolation.

To illustrate the development process at United Airlines, the Flight Operations Training program modules were made up in a draft form and inserted in PLATO learning management. Once in the system, authors, as well as

Figure 22

Planning Documents

I.U.			LIBRARY RESOURCES	
Objective	Test Item	Text Reference	Workbook Learning Activity	PLATO Learning Activity
11.1	1 2	S. 58-63	Economics Student Manual pp. 1-3	obj. 1 obj. 3
11.2	3 4 5	S. 63-64	4	obj. 4
11.3	14	S. 64-65	5-6	obj. 5
11.4	9	S. 65-67	7	—
11.5	10	S. 67-68	8	—
11.6	11 12	S. 381-386	9-11	obj. 8
11.7	13	S. 386-388	12-14	obj. 9
11.8	6 7	S. 387-388	15-16	obj. 10
11.9	8	S. 389-391	17	obj. 11
11.10	15 16	S. 391-399	18	—
Overview Workbook Review Activity - Economics Student Manual pp. 19-28 PLATO Review Activity - ?				

students, were able to provide commentary to assist in the refining of course material. The CMI structure enables United to implement a course very rapidly. In the developmental effort at The American College, draft objectives, test items, and learning resources were inserted in the computer. Because of the developmental nature of the work, considerable reliance was placed upon student feedback in moving from the original draft version to the final copy.

VI.

RESOURCES

Further information on PLATO can be obtained from Control Data Learning Centers. Learning Centers can be found in most major cities of the United States.

Information about the following materials may also be obtained from:

Control Data Corporation
P.O. Box O
Minneapolis, Minnesota 55440

- *Introduction to TUTOR,* James R. Ghesquiere, Celia R. Davis, and Charlene A. Thompson
- *The TUTOR Language,* Bruce A. Sherwood
- *Control Data PLATO System Overview*
- *PLATO Author Language Reference Manual*
- *PLATO Author Language Instruction Formats Pocket References*
- *Control Data PLATO CMI System Overview*
- *PLATO CMI Author's Guide*
- *PLATO CMI Instructor's Guide*

Further information on PLATO learning management can be obtained from:

Michael W. Allen, Ph.D.
Principal Consultant
CBE Development Division

Control Data Corporation
8120 Penn Avenue South
Suite 435
Minneapolis, Minnesota 55431

SELECTED REFERENCES

Alderman, D.L., Appel, L.R., and Murphy, R.T. PLATO and TICCIT. An Evaluation of CAI in the Community College. *Educational Technology,* April 1978, *18* (4), 40-45.

Buchanan, C. Results of One Year of Computer-Based Instruction at the United Airlines Flight Operations Training Center. Proceedings of the 1979 Convention of the Association for the Development of Computer-Based Instructional Systems, 377-393.

Nelson, C.D., Lavanhar, P., and Pepper, G. Sex Education on PLATO. Proceedings of the 1979 Convention of the Association for the Development of Computer-Based Instructional Systems, 959-975.

Nichols, R.D. The PLATO Display in the Teaching of Optical Letter-Spacing. Proceedings of the 1979 Convention of the Association for the Development of Computer-Based Instructional Systems, 1022-1026.

Nichols, R.D., and Wickham, C. PLATO in the Teaching of Foundation Visual Design. Proceedings of the 1979 Convention of the Association for the Development of Computer-Based Instructional Systems, 986-989.

Rebstock, T., and Harkey, J.C. PLATO Simulation for Process Operator Training. Proceedings of the 1979 Convention of the Association for the Development of Computer-Based Instructional Systems, 976-985.

Siegel, M.A., and Simutis, Z.M. CAI for Adult Basic Skills Training: Two Applications. Proceedings of the 1979 Convention of the Association for the Development of Computer-Based Instructional Systems, 991-1004.

Stifle, J., Smith, S., and Andersen, D. Microprocessor Delivery of PLATO Courseware. Proceedings of the 1979 Convention of the Association for the Development of Computer-Based Instructional Systems, 1027-1035.

VII.

APPENDIX

For the past 20 years, researchers at the University of Illinois have been working on the development of an educational system that is at once individualized, adaptable, efficient, reliable, and cost-effective. Educators at the University of Illinois Computer-based Education Research Laboratory (CERL), working under the direction of Donald Bitzer, have used the technological capabilities of the computer to develop a sophisticated and efficient learning system known as PLATO.

CERL believed that computers would make excellent teaching aids because of their ability to offer individualized learning experiences. Students could proceed through learning materials at their own comfortable pace, repeating any material which they found difficult and skipping any material which they already knew. Interaction with the computer would involve the student and thus hold his or her interest longer, while the feedback made possible by the computer would facilitate learning. Advanced recordkeeping capabilities would permit a teacher to assess his or her students' progress in great detail, while freeing a significant portion of the teacher's time for other educational activities and individual tutoring.

CERL's first attempt at computer-assisted education, in 1960, known as PLATO I, used a high-speed digital computer attached to a student terminal. This single student station was attached to an Illiac I which provided drill and practice and basic tutorial lessons.

In the next few years, CERL turned its attention to the addition of a second interactive student terminal to a single computer. To facilitate multiple users, the Illiac I was replaced by a Control Data 1604 computer, and this phase of the computer-based education project became known as PLATO II.

The development of PLATO III in 1964 offered a number of significant advances over earlier generations of computer-based education. The capacity of a single Control Data 1604 had been expanded so that one computer could now support 20 student terminals, and communication capabilities had been added so that students could contact their instructors, and developers could share information among one another. In addition to drill and tutorial lessons previously available, PLATO III could support a wide variety of instructional strategies, including lessons utilizing the inquiry method, dialogues, simulations, games, and problem-solving. More sophisticated student response judging allowed PLATO to evaluate multiple-word student responses, as well as giving cues indicating words in the student's response that were misspelled, incorrect, or out of order. PLATO III also contained a number of innovations designed to benefit lesson authors and instructors. The development of the *PLATO Author Language Reference Manual* made it possible for subject-matter experts with no previous computer experience to write their own PLATO lessons without the aid of a programmer. Furthermore, since PLATO was now capable of recording every key-press of a student's response, lesson authors could collect data on student performance that would be invaluable in revising their lessons, while permitting instructors to track their students' progress through PLATO course material.

Appendix

In 1972, CERL and Control Data Corporation felt that the PLATO system was effective enough to be offered on a national basis in its latest form, PLATO IV. PLATO IV terminals were connected to a powerful Control Data Cyber 73-24 computer and featured a plasma display screen which could be activated by students' touch responses as well as containing the capability for random-access microfiche projection on the same display as the computer output. The new terminals could now be connected to the main computer by conventional phone lines; and, as a result, 400 PLATO terminals were in operation at 70 different locations by the winter of 1974. A single computer main-frame could now serve these several hundred terminals scattered all over the United States, teaching different lessons simultaneously throughout the country.

In 1976, Control Data Corporation announced its intention to market computer-based education via PLATO to business and industry for training functions, an area of education not previously served by PLATO. Working with CERL at the University of Illinois, Control Data is continuing to refine and implement PLATO in order to enhance educational opportunities for students of all levels throughout the country.

HAROLD F. RAHMLOW is Professor of Education, The American College, Bryn Mawr, Pennsylvania. He holds B.S. and M.S. degrees from the University of the Pacific and a Ph.D. from Washington State University. Prior to joining the College, he was a Principal Research Scientist with the American Institutes for Research, Palo Alto, California, where he was instrumental in the development of Project PLAN. Dr. Rahmlow is currently responsible for the College's computer-based education research and development program, which includes PLATO activities. He is a frequent speaker, writer, and consultant on computer-based education.

ROBERT C. FRATINI is a Technical Training Associate at the Western Electric Bell System Training Center in Dublin, Ohio, specializing in the design and development of computer-based training. From 1975 to 1979, he was an Instructional Design Specialist for The American College, where he was instrumental in the development of materials using the PLATO system. He holds an M.S. in Instructional Media and Design from Pennsylvania State University and a B.A. from Trinity College, Hartford, Connecticut.

JAMES R. GHESQUIERE has been involved in computer-based instruction in a number of capacities during the past ten years. While at the University of Illinois, he co-authored *Introduction to TUTOR*, wrote a reference manual on the PLATO system, and managed a group of PLATO consultants. In his current position with Control Data Corporation, Dr. Ghesquiere manages a group of instructional analysts who are developing PLATO courseware for business, industry, and government agencies.